TEACHABLE MOMENTS

Teaching Children How to
Remember God's Truth

Kent McClain

destinēe

519

TEACHABLE MOMENTS
Teaching Children How to Remember God's Truth
By Kent McClain

Copyright © 2012 Kent McClain
ISBN: 978-1-938367-01-4
Publication date: 2012
Published by Destinée Media: www.destineemedia.com
Cover design: Scott Davis www.scottdaviscreative.com
Interior design: Per-Ole Lind www.perolelind.com
Interior layout: Ralph McCall
Set with Bembo and Akzidenz-Grotesk BQ

To Myrna

Great wife

Devoted mother

Loving grandmother

Dedicated daughter

Hard worker

and

Unwavering Christian

WITH GRATITUDE

I want to thank all of those who took my manuscript and fine-tuned it with their editing skills, biblical insight, and wise suggestions. These special people in my life include: Wendell Wellman (Hollywood screen writer, college roommate, and friend for over 45 years), Kathy Dunkin (school teacher, caring parent, who edited as she fought cancer), Brodie McClain (pastor, missionary, loving parent, who has so wonderfully filled the role of son), Shannon Allen (realtor, dedicated wife, short-term missionary, and the daughter of my heart), Kelli Brown (school staff editor and grammatical genius), Ralph McCall (author, publisher, parent, and great friend who during our first basketball game gave me such a blow to the head that I had to have stitches), and Myrna McClain (school teacher, devoted parent and grandparent, and continuous encourager in the loving role as wife).

Finally, a great deal of appreciation and gratitude goes to many friends, and my family, Jerry, Susanne, mom, Nic, Katie, and my three wonderful grandchildren, Luke, Maddie, and Anabelle. All encouraged, supported, and prayed for me as I wrote Teachable Moments.

CONTENTS

Section III: The 'P' in the TIPS for Parenting   105

PREFACE

Train up a child in the way he should go, even when he is old he will not depart from it.   *(Proverbs 22:6)*

It was the last inning of the game, and it looked like my Pantry Market baseball team was going to win the Pasadena Little League Championship of 1957. I remember how challenging the game had been, because even though I was a good hitter, I was unable to run the bases very well. I had a bicycle accident the day before and could hardly round first base at more than a fast walk no matter how hard I hit the ball. In the end, we won, and that made it a good day.

I remember how thrilled all the parents were as they got into their cars to take their kids out for special dinners and treats afterward. Seeing that I was alone, some had asked that I join them. I decided not to go along; instead, getting on my bike and peddling home thinking of all the crazy plays that made a difference in the game.

Playing sports was very important to me when I was young. Yet, sadly, I don't remember either of my parents attending my games. Of course, they had their challenges as young parents. My dad was a busy pastor, but it was not his many church duties that kept him away from my games. It was his quick exit from the family after having an affair with a church secretary. I was only six at the time, so I hardly got to know him before he was gone; I rarely saw him again until my college years. My mom, to her credit, though, wanted to be at my games but was quite overwhelmed with being a single parent. Much of her time during those early years was spent working two jobs and providing a home for my brother and me.

So, I rode off that day after the game, happy we had won but a bit sad that once again no one had been there yelling things like, "Way to go, Kent; nice play; good job; good boy!"

As I grew older, I got over these disappointments and settled for the joys of playing well or hearing encouraging comments from fellow teammates and their parents. It wasn't until one Saturday morning at my own son's first soccer game that all of this came back to me, but in a wonderful way. He was seven years old; close to the age I was when I got involved in sports.

Brodie's game took place in Colorado during my first year as Senior Pastor of a small church. The game was exciting as I recall. Brodie played goalie and did a good job blocking one goal attempt after another. Parents on both sides were applauding, clapping, and yelling encouragements to their children. The game ended in a tie, and everyone gathered around their sons commending each for their good play. My wife, Myrna, and I did the same and even promised our son an immediate trip to McDonalds to get anything he wanted. As we were walking off the field, tears began to well up within, tears I let no one see. They were tears of joy because I was able to be there for Brodie. As much as I thought it would be great to have my parents at my games rooting me on, it seemed now even greater to be there for my son's games and later for my daughter's. Over the years, I often wondered if being there had made a difference in my children's lives, and when Brodie's days of team sports ended, I got an answer.

When Brodie was in college, his volleyball team was playing in the championships at the University of Texas. His team did well during the whole tournament, even defeating the previous national champions to get to the semi-finals. They ended up losing the semi-final game, but his team from Washington State University placed third, the best they had ever done. On the flight home the next morning, Brodie turned to me and said, "Dad, thanks for always being there for me, all the games, all the practices; I'll never forget it."

As heartwarming as that experience turned out, even greater joy came when both my children grasped the Christian life and lived it amongst their friends and peers during their years at home. Even in college, when many young people abandon their beliefs and standards, both Brodie and Shannon stayed true to theirs, even sharing Christ with others on two very secular campuses.

They were not perfect kids, by any means, nor were Myrna and I perfect parents. Mistakes were many, frustrations occurred often, and challenges arose. As parents we struggled and often felt inadequate to the task of raising our children. Our flaws and weaknesses were evident throughout our parenting.

Yet, despite those faults and weaknesses and aside from the loving relationship we pursued with our children, we made a sincere effort to help them understand God and the world in which they lived. Teaching them the Scriptures so they would always remember them, using what I call *Teachable Moments (Teaching Children How to Remember God's Truth)*, was important. The Scriptures not only provided critical principles, truths, and guidelines to follow, they also helped establish within each of us minds and hearts desiring God.

Some of what Myrna and I experienced as parents is in this book, which I have called Teachable Moments. However, a great deal of what follows comes from the experiences we had with other parents and children. It was actually their questions, problems, challenges, and frustrations that pushed me to study the Scripture in regard to parenting. As a result, I believe I found some biblical answers, patterns, and possible blueprints to follow in parenting; ones that may help you have a wonderful and rewarding experience with your children. If you follow every suggestion in this book and do every Teachable Moment, will you be a perfect parent? Will you have perfect children? No! The goal of the book is not perfect parents or perfect children, but parents and children attuned to God's voice and leading.

God speed as you read through *Teachable Moments*. When you are finished, may the Scriptures be what you remember most, for all other books, including this one, pale in comparison to them.

Kent McClain

INTRODUCTION

(Discipling and teaching children so they always remember)

…Observe the commandment of your father and do not forsake the teaching of your mother; bind them continually on your heart; tie them around your neck. When you walk about, they will guide you; when you sleep, they will watch over you; and when you awake, they will talk to you.
(Proverbs 6:20-22)

What do I do when my children disobey, rebel, or do things that are hurtful to others? Do I spank them, give them grace, or try and do a little of each? And when trying to balance the two, how do I determine which and when, and how much to apply?

So many "Christian" children, even pastors' kids, falter as they get older. What can I do so my children don't do the same?

How can my children remember the great truths of Scripture so that when they really need it, when they have to make those tough decisions in life by themselves, they will have these truths from which to draw?

The world is so raunchy and evil at times, how do I protect my kids from it? Do I force them to go to church, or put them in a Christian school to be safe? And if I do, who ministers to those children out there in the world who need the Lord?

How do I build loving relationships with my children, so that when I give them advice or share God's truth, they will listen to me?

These are just a few of the perplexing questions parents have asked me over the years, queries that pushed me to write *Teachable Moments*. I began work on this book in 1998, and 14 years later it is complete. It took so long because the Lord put on my heart from the very beginning to back everything with Scripture. Therefore, as much as possible, *Teachable Moments* reflects what the Scripture says about parenting, if not directly, then at least in a related way. As you read it though, please grant me a measure of grace, because as much as I tried to support every thought with Scripture, I am sure my own opinions seep through from time to time.

The first two of the 14 years of writing was spent reading and cataloguing every verse in the Bible from Genesis to Revelation. Each was looked at in respect to its possible relevance and application to parenting and raising children. Two more years were taken to organize and arrange those notes into a sequence of chapters. The final ten years were devoted to writing and integrating the Scripture with my own experiences as a parent, grandparent, pastor, assistant pastor, youth minister, children and family life minister, Christian school superintendent, teacher, and coach.

Focus

The focus of *Teachable Moments* and its companion book *Sowing Teachable Moments Year One,* is three-fold, to help you teach your children the Word in such a way they will always remember it, to help you direct their hearts toward God and others, and to disciple them the way Jesus did. The use of vivid illustration, or what I call "Teachable Moments," will be emphasized from the beginning to the end of this book. Jesus was a great example of this style of teaching, as was proven by many of His parables, analogies, and comparisons when revealing truth. To help change your children's hearts, building a close and loving relationship with them is very important, as presented throughout the section on Intimacy. And discipling your children the way God (Trinity) did in the Old Testament, and Jesus did in the New Testament, is essential if they are to become who God created them to be.

Underlying Themes

While pursuing the Scriptures as the primary resource for *Teachable Moments,* two underlying themes came to light that impacted the entire core of this book. The first was God's role as a parent which He demonstrated throughout Scripture. In each generation, whether the first with Adam and Eve or midstream with Paul and the other founders of the early church, God's parenting expertise was evident as He raised His children, mankind. Because of this, many of His practices and principles, whether from the Old or New Testaments, are applicable to parenting. *Teachable Moments* cites several of these throughout.

The second theme pioneers the idea that there are general patterns and answers in Scripture to follow when disciplining children. This whole issue has perplexed and troubled many parents because of the many conflicting opinions expressed, even amongst Christians. Add to this the views of the so called world professionals in child rearing, and you have an even greater tangled web when it comes to knowing what to do when correcting your children. Yet, the Scripture puts forth some great guidelines to ground parents in this area. These guidelines are detailed in Chapters 9: The Rod of Discipline and 10: The Staff of Grace, Mercy, and Forgiveness.

The Name

Years ago when I first began writing parenting articles that focused on how parents could disciple their children, I chose *Teachable Moments* for my overarching title. It was a title I took from a pastor friend of mine who often associated Scriptural truth in his preaching to what he saw everyday. And since a great part of this book, and the one that follows, deals with how to teach your children so they always remember God's truth, *Teachable Moments* became the name.

Organization

Teachable Moments has four parts, which I call TIPS in parenting. The T in this acronym stands for **teaching** your children the Word. The I represents building **intimate** relationships with your children. The P symbolizes **preparing** your children to handle the world and their own futures ahead. And the S stands for **sowing** 24 teachable moments into their lives, lessons in the Word they will never forget.

Teachable Moments and its four parts is actually broken down into two books. This book deals with the first three parts of TIPS, teaching, intimacy building, and preparing your children for the world and future. The second book, *Sowing Teachable Moments Year* One is a companion book to this one, and it deals with the S in the TIPS. Within it are 24 different Teachable Moment activities you can do with your children.

At the end of most chapters in this book are suggested Teachable Moments to help you remember what was emphasized. These were included to show you how practical and easy it is to create a Teachable Moment. If you can do this for yourself, then you will have no problem doing it with your children.

In each chapter the Trinity (God the Father, Son, Spirit), or Jesus in particular, provides the first foundational insight. Then others like David, Peter, and Paul are brought in from either the Old or New Testaments. The Trinity or Jesus Himself models perfect understanding, thinking, and doing when it comes to parenting. David, Peter, and the other biblical figures give you insight into parenting from a saved, yet still sinful state, like the one from which you and I are coming. *(Romans 7: 14-17)*

Although there are probably less than a hundred direct verses or passages of Scripture that deal specifically with parenting in the Bible, there are thousands of others that can be applied. To cite many of these in *Teachable Moments*, I have referenced them in parenthesis at the end of sentences. They follow the ending punctuation because in many cases the references typically apply to more than one preceding thought or sentence.

The Scriptures used throughout the book were primarily from the New American Standard Version of the Bible. The final count in the book ended up to be over 1100 verses in 422 passages.

Some of the Scriptural quotes were shortened for the sake of space. When I did this, I either put three periods in a row in a verse to alert you that some words had been taken out, or I put the abbreviation rbk at the end, standing for revised by Kent. In doing this, I made every effort not to change the meaning of the verses or passages.

Lastly, some of the names in the stories and anecdotes throughout the book have been changed. This was done to protect their identity. In saying this, though, each story is true at its core; only some details were added or changed when certain ones could not be remembered, or when two or more stories were combined.

Final Thoughts

While writing *Teachable Moments* and *Sowing Teachable Moments Year One*, I had the spiritual development of your children in mind, but I also had you, the parent in my sight, perhaps even more so. For I believe that if you apply *Teachable Moments* with your children, God will let your discipleship spill over to other parents, children, neighbors, fellow workers, and family members. And of course your children will likely do the same with their own children one day, as well as their friends and acquaintances along the way. Wouldn't that be great!

Teachable Moment

Blessed is the man who trusts in the Lord and whose trust is the Lord. For he will be like a tree planted by the water, that extends its roots by a stream and will not fear when the heat comes; but its leaves will be green, and it will not be anxious in a year of drought nor cease to yield fruit. (Jeremiah 17:7-8)

At my wife's childhood home, which sat on ten acres near a small creek, there stood a grove of walnut trees her dad planted. He was a doctor but enjoyed the diversion and recreation of planting trees and farming.

In the middle of one of his biggest fields sitting directly in front of the house, stood a huge walnut tree, much like the tree pictured on the cover of this book. It was magnificent because of the root system it developed over the years; no storm had ever been able to knock it over or do much damage to its main branches. My wife loved this tree, because it was great to play under and on as a child. Her dad, whom she loved deeply, even attached a rope to one of its branches so she could swing on it to her heart's delight. The tree remained for years, even through Myrna's college days, first years of marriage, and the early raising of our children. When our young family used to visit her parents, this majestic tree seemingly was the first thing that caught her eye when turning the last corner to the house. As we traveled down the long driveway, I often looked over to see Myrna gazing at it with a contented smile on her face. I'm sure as she looked the old tree brought back wonderful memories of her childhood.

For this Teachable Moment illustration you need to find a similar tree, perhaps like the one on the cover of this book that will help you remember the kind of parent God wants you to be. One who is well rooted in His Word and thus able to give your children biblical answers to life's questions.

The tree should remind you to be strong in character, opting for what is right, especially in your children's presence. Its ability to stay standing through one storm after the next should remind you to depend on Him in all circumstances, not just for your own sake, but for your family's. The tree's shielding branches should remind you of the constant protection God wants you to provide for your children. Finally, the produce or leaves of the tree ought to remind you of the world's need for the truth about God that should always fall from your branches.

The following verses referenced in this chapter can be found in sequence on my web site, www.tmoments.com. Click on the Book Resources button located on the home page.

Romans 7:14-17

 I

The T in TIPS for Parenting

(The importance and best way of teaching when discipling your children)

Hear, my son, your father's instruction, and do not forsake your mother's teaching; indeed, they are a graceful wreath to your head.
(Proverbs 1:8-9)

This section is based on **202** verses in **73** passages of Scripture.

Thoughts ahead

My only regret is that I wish I could have learned what I did much earlier, when I was a child. But, better late than never! Chapter 1

Fat may not always be a good thing in respect to health, but it is a good thing in regard to teaching your children the Word. Chapter 2

Eventually your children will become more abstract thinkers as they grow older, but until then, concrete teaching (Teachable Moments) will speak the loudest and longest to them. So when you are teaching your children the Word, make sure an illustration goes with what you are teaching. Chapter 3

ONE
COUNTS COUNTED

(The importance of teaching your children the Word)

Your word is a lamp to my feet and a light to my path. I will never forget Your precepts, for by them You have revived me. I understand more than the aged, because I have observed them.

(Psalm 119:105, 93, 100)

If you really intend to raise your children as best you can and disciple them as God would have, then teaching them the Word is the first of four vital keys. It is the **T** in my acronym TIPS for parenting. The **I** stands for building intimacy between you and your children, the **P** for their preparation, and the **S** for sowing in them memorable lessons, which is in the companion book, *Sowing Teachable Moments Year One*.

Before unveiling the particulars of teaching the Word, let me share with you a personal story where I benefited greatly from the teaching of another at a very important time in my life. **My only regret is that I wish I could have learned what I did much earlier, when I was a child. But, better late than never!**

It was 1969, and I had just finished the first year of my Master's Degree program at the University of Wyoming. I had spent a challenging year taking some very difficult graduate classes. My major was Communication Theory, a cross between rhetoric, communication, and philosophy. As hard as these studies were, they paled in comparison to the demands on my faith that first year at Wyoming. It was midnight after my last day of classes that year when I decided to take off for home in my surfer-looking VW bus. I could hardly wait to get back home, especially to the warm weather and beaches of Southern California. Needless to say, attending school in Wyoming was quite a contrast to living in Southern California. It was very beautiful there, though, even when twenty below zero.

As I got on the I-80 headed for home, I had plenty of time to reflect on what I had experienced at school, because my radio was broken. For the next 20 or so hours I had only my thoughts and the Lord to listen to. Hour after hour I thought of all I had experienced during this first year. As the journey wore on, I grew confused and unsettled in my spirit because there was too much of a mixture of spiritual victories and *fleshly* defeats. Some things I felt good about, like sharing the Gospel with several students and two campus fraternities with the aid of Campus Crusade for Christ. But then there were other things I did that I wish I hadn't, like drinking too much on certain occasions. As I reflect now, I attribute the poor decisions I made to three factors: disobedience to the Scriptural truths I knew, a lack of biblical knowledge in several areas of the Bible, and a complete misunderstanding of God's grace. Although I had grown up in a very evangelistic church and attended a Christian College, I somehow came up short in my knowledge of the Word and faith, especially when it counted.

After crossing into California later the next day, I felt a great relief to finally be near home, but wondered how I could return to Wyoming for my final year feeling the way I did. As I arrived in L.A. that evening, instead of going home I headed over to the Jesus Christ Light and Power House, a popular college Bible study that met in an old fraternity house at UCLA. I went there first because I knew from the summer before they met that evening. I also knew there was a strong possibility my brother, Jerry, and his wife Susanne, would be there, for they sometimes helped with the music when they weren't on the road entertaining. If you have ever heard the song, "Happy Days," then you have heard Jerry and his group.

When I arrived, the place was packed. Instead of 100 college students like the summer before, there were six to seven hundred filling every room and hallway in the house. Wow! I couldn't believe there were so many interested in the Bible. And sure enough as I walked in, my brother and his wife were leading the music. When they saw me, they stopped everything for a moment to give me a hug.

After the meeting my brother and I immediately connected, for we had always been very close, especially after our parents divorced. Before I could open my mouth, he said, "You're staying with Susanne and I, and that's all there is to it." I had no temptation to say otherwise, so I accepted and moved in with them for the summer. After the first few days of being together with them, they asked why I was so down. I explained some of the struggles I'd had at school, issues I had thought about during the long drive home. Both listened, but felt Bill Counts, one of the teachers at the Jesus Christ Light and Power House and past leaders of Campus Crusade for Christ, could help me most. Since Jerry knew Bill very well, he set up a meeting between the two of us.

In that first meeting, Bill detected right away how little I knew about certain parts of the Bible, especially issues dealing with God's grace, love, and forgiveness. And even though he was always in demand to speak here and there, he committed to meeting with me one-on-one throughout the summer, just to teach me the Scripture. All I can say is this was one of the best summers I'd had in a long time, and when it came time to go back to Wyoming I was very much encouraged and spiritually enlivened. My second and last year at Wyoming ended up to be a great one, particularly in respect to understanding the Word and doing God's will.

Bill continued to have an input on my life long after my days at Wyoming. He took me on some of his speaking trips where he introduced me to other Christian leaders. On one of our flights home, I asked him why he took me along, for it was at his expense. He said, "Kent, it's time you see what other Christian leaders are thinking and doing; you can learn a lot from them about God's Word and how it can be lived." I was surprised at what he said, but now as I look back, I realize that aside from being such a good teacher, Bill was very humble, a quality I often found accompanying those who were good teachers of the Word.

Bill's story, in so many ways represents much of what this section on teaching is about. He loved God's Word, felt it could change a life, was willing to take time with others to teach it, and humbly lived his own life by its precepts. Because of this Bill Counts life counted, just as yours will too, if you likewise teach your children the Word.

What's Ahead?

This teaching section consists of two chapters called *FAT Is Good,* and *The Marriage Cup.* In these chapters, the importance of the Word, its power to change a child's life, what it takes to teach it, and how you can make it memorable will be covered.

The Biblical Examples

In order to gain a Scriptural perspective, Peter, the entire Godhead (Father, Son, and Spirit) of the Old Testament, and Jesus in the New, will be the primary biblical figures from which truth is drawn. Peter was chosen for good reasons: for one, he was a forgiven sinner like you and I, and therefore easy to relate to. For another he was a good teacher as his letters prove and actions show throughout the book of Acts. *(Mark 8:32-33; Acts 4:8-12)*

The Godhead (Trinity) was chosen to show that teaching with visible illustration (Teachable Moments) was not only a style of teaching Jesus employed, it was used from the very beginning to explain and visualize truth.

Final Thoughts

In addition to Bill Counts there were others God sent to me throughout my life. Each helped me understand God's truth and how to live the Christian life. As I mentioned earlier, I came from a broken home, so I needed all the help I could get. God sent my way Sunday school teachers, public school teachers, church youth directors, and friends who loved the Lord. In the end each made their own impact and contribution, as you will too with your children as you teach and disciple them.

The following verses referenced in this chapter can be found in sequence on my web site, www.tmoments.com. Click on the Book Resources button located on the home page.

Mark 8:32-33; Acts 4:8-12

TWO

FAT IS GOOD

(Qualifications for teaching)

These words, which I am commanding you today, shall be on your heart. You shall teach them diligently to your sons and shall talk of them when you sit in your house and when you walk by the way and when you lie down and when you rise up.   *(Deuteronomy 6:6-7)*

If you grasp the importance of teaching God's Word to your children early in parenting, then you have taken a big step toward preparing them for the world. For the Word will equip them with the skills to think and act according to God's plans and aspirations. It will greatly aid your children into becoming good decision–makers now and in the future.

When you grasp how powerful the Word is when imbedded in your children's hearts, then you have also taken a big step to empower them to do just about anything. For with the Word comes the presence and power of the Spirit as Paul writes to the Ephesians:

Now we have received, not the spirit of the world, but the Spirit who is from God, so that we may know the things freely given to us by God, which things we also speak, not in words taught by human wisdom, but in those taught by the Spirit, combining spiritual thoughts with spiritual words. (I Corinthians 2:12-13)

If you grasp how attainable God has made it for you to teach your children, I doubt you will hesitate to begin immediately if you haven't already. For not only will it be rewarding for you, it accomplishes God's desire to have your children equipped with the tools to make them spiritually and emotionally strong.

In the following examples of Peter and Jesus, many principles will be discussed to help you teach the Word to your children.

Peter

Peter was one of the best teachers in the New Testament, in part because he had a working knowledge of the Old Testament. He gained this by growing up in a Jewish home which usually honored and taught the Old Testament, along with many other associated laws and customs. He also spent three-and-a-half years with Jesus, learning great depth and understanding of the Scripture.

However, perhaps the most important reasons Peter became such a good teacher were due to his faithfulness, availability, and teachable spirit. In respect to his faithfulness, He was willing to lay everything aside to follow Christ, even his own livelihood of fishing. *(Luke 5:4-11; Matthew 19:27-29)* In regard to availability, Peter taught whenever and wherever God asked. His teaching to thousands at Pentecost was an example of this, which was not long after running for cover when Jesus was put on trial. *(Acts 2:14-17; 21-22, 32-33, 37-38, 40-41)* Finally, Peter was very teachable, always willing to learn more, not just from Jesus, but later from others like Paul. This was remarkable because Paul had not been with Jesus the way Peter had. Yet, Peter respected Paul's teaching and even his rebukes on his thinking. There were two occasions where this was evident; one was recorded in the book of Galatians where Paul reproved Peter for living like a grace-filled Gentile Christian, but telling others to live like a law-oriented Jew. To Peter's credit he received Paul's rebuke with humility and stopped. *(Galatians 2:14)* The other occasion was in Acts 15 where Peter listened to Paul's argument against requiring circumcision for a Gentile's faith. Peter agreed while proclaiming Paul's wisdom on the matter as the right perspective, for it was to be based on faith, and faith alone. *(Acts 15:3-6, 7-11)* In these instances, and perhaps many others, Peter could have balked at Paul, but didn't because of his humble and teachable spirit, an important factor in teaching. Having a humble attitude is something to keep in mind when teaching your children, for they will likely listen to you better if you too have such a spirit.

Jesus

Teaching the Word to others was extremely important to Jesus because it communicated the Father's, Spirit's, and His perspective on the matters of life, particularly in respect to choice making. The disciples, with the exception of Judas, testify to this, for what Jesus taught them changed their perspective as well as their entire lives. *(Mark 1:14-22)* It led them to accept Him as Lord and Savior, to become disciples, and then Apostles. This was quite a change for Andrew, James, and John, who likely would have continued as fishermen had they not heard the truth and responded. *(Luke 9:1-2; Acts 4: 13)*

In addition to these changes, Jesus' teaching also equipped the disciples to share the Word with others. In preparing them, Jesus made Himself accessible and very available.

He availed Himself for several reasons, perhaps foremost to change and reform what they knew and didn't know about truth and Scripture. Like many Jews of their day, the disciples knew partially about God because He had given their nation His teachings, laws, and revelations first. *(Romans 1:15-17; Romans 3:1-2)* This was encapsulated in what we know as the Old Testament.

By making Himself available to the disciples, Jesus was able to spend as much time as it took to teach and correct what they knew about God's truth. For like so many others of their day, the disciples had been wrongly led and taught by the religious leaders. *(Matthew 23:13; Matthew 9:34-35)* The extra time resulting from His availability also opened the door for four important things to occur. First, it allowed Jesus to repeat many teachings which may have not been fully grasped. Second, it gave the disciples a chance to ask questions and pose concerns. Third, it gave the disciples the opportunity to see Jesus live out truth in their presence. And fourth, it gave them several occasions to try out what He had taught them. The following are examples of these four aspects.

A repeated teaching on prayer

But I say to you, love your enemies and pray for those who persecute you. (Matthew 5:44)

It happened that while Jesus was praying in a certain place, after He had finished, one of His disciples said to Him, "Lord, teach us to pray just as John also taught his disciples." And He said to them, "When you pray, say: 'Father, hallowed be Your name. Your kingdom come. Give us each day our daily bread. And forgive us our sins, for we ourselves also forgive everyone who is indebted to us. And lead us not into temptation." (Luke 11:1-4)

Ask, and it will be given to you; seek, and you will find; knock, and it will be opened to you. (Matthew 7: 7)

Disciple's questions and concerns

Then Peter came and said to Him, "Lord, how often shall my brother sin against me and I forgive him? Up to seven times?" (Matthew 18:21)

When He got into the boat, His disciples followed Him. And behold, there arose a great storm on the sea, so that the boat was being covered with the waves; but Jesus Himself was asleep. And they came to Him and woke Him, saying, "Save us, Lord; we are perishing! He said to them, "Why are you afraid, you men of little faith?" Then He got up and rebuked the winds and the sea, and it became perfectly calm. The men were amazed, and said, "What kind of a man is this, that even the winds and the sea obey Him?" (Matthew 8:23-27)

Jesus' living out of truth:

And He withdrew from them about a stone's throw, and He knelt down and began to pray, saying, "Father, if You are willing, remove this cup from Me; yet not My will, but Yours be done." And being in agony He was praying very fervently; and His sweat became like drops of blood, falling down upon the ground. (Luke 22:41-42, 44)

Applying what they had learned:

When the disciples saw Him walking on the sea, they were terrified, and said, "It is a ghost!" And they cried out in fear. But immediately Jesus spoke to them, saying, "Take courage, it is I; do not be afraid." Peter said to Him, "Lord, if it is You, command me to come to You on the water." And He said, "Come!" And Peter got out of the boat, and walked on the water and came toward Jesus. But seeing the wind, he became frightened, and beginning to sink, he cried out, "Lord, save me!" Immediately Jesus stretched out His hand and took hold of him, and said to him, "You of little faith, why did you doubt?" (Matthew 14:26-31)

Lastly, in the approximately 1200 days Jesus spent with the disciples, He faithfully taught as much as He could to them, a goal you might keep in mind while raising your children. Included were scores of lessons. In a book I wrote on discipleship several years ago called *Mission Possible*, I noted that during His first 18 months with the disciples, He either taught or modeled over 142 lessons.[1]

In conclusion, Jesus covered a lot with the disciples in a short time, as you will too during the course of your children's lifetime.

Parent Application

To help you teach your children the Word, here are some thoughts, guidelines, and practical applications under the following headings: *Preparing to Teach, Falling in Love with the Word, Results of not Being Taught Well, The Power Behind the Word,* and *Prerequisites for Teaching.*

Preparing to Teach

When my kids became teenagers, they sometimes made fun of me for overdoing it when it came to preparing our car for long trips during the summer. But experience taught me that anything can happen during the course of a trip, so I did everything possible to account for all of those possibilities. I began by having my car serviced (oil, oil filter, tire pressure, battery, etc.), connected up my CB radio (no cell phones back then), replaced the windshield wipers, made sure the spare tire had air, put in extra food, clothes, and blankets, upgraded the medical kit, and took along extra water, peanut butter, honey, and tools to fix any radiator problems. I could go on, but I think you get the idea of my preparation. I am glad to say that in all of our trips, there wasn't a problem that delayed us long from our destination.

Preparing your children with the Word is similar in that you prepare them with all the biblical teaching you can so that they will be able to face all that the world will throw at them. This includes giving them a biblical perspective on choosing the right friends, turning away from worldly temptations, doing what is best, loving others, and even choosing a life's mate one day, to name a few.

Now, you may question whether you are capable of preparing your children for all that is out there in the world, after all there are so many challenges. Then there is the reality that not many parents today are successful keeping their children unstained from the world's influence. But realize this: you have Christ within to help you do every part of what you need to do to prepare your children. *(Galatians 2:20)* And just as He poured Himself into the disciples, so He will with your children if you let Him. *(Romans 10:17)* All you need do is recognize His presence and put your faith in Him. In response, He will do things through your teaching that you could never have thought possible.

Falling in Love with the Word

Often a great test of whether you really love something or not is how much time and effort you put into it. You usually love something that is fulfilling, uplifting, or enjoyable. I loved sports because it gave me these feelings and experiences. It stood to reason that when my kids came along, I wanted them to experience the same. I told Brodie and Shannon on more than one occasion that it would take a lot of practice and dedication to become good in their sports. But I did more than that; I taught them strategies and practiced with them hour after hour, and year after year. The more they practiced the better they got, which led them to develop a great love for their sports, especially when they won.

As great a love as our family had for sports, the love we developed for the Scripture as we studied it together was exceedingly more influential. In fact there is no comparison, for unlike sports, the Scripture gave us thousands, if not tens of thousands of lasting encouragements and answers to life with God. The more we read and discussed the Word together, the more we fell in love with it, because it unfailingly met each of our needs. Today my kids are gone, developing families of their own. What isn't gone, though, is our continuing love for the Word, which still permeates our thoughts and conversations when we get together.

Peter deeply loved the Word because it gave him the answers to life and revealed what God thought of him and others who believed.

But the Word of the Lord endures forever, and this is the Word which was preached to you. (I Peter 1:25)

This precious value, then, is for you who believe… you are a chosen race, a royal priesthood, a holy nation, a people for God's own possession, so that you may proclaim the excellencies of Him who has called you out of darkness into His marvelous light. (I Peter 2:7, 9)

Peter also loved the Word because in so many other instances it met his needs and renewed his hope. Perhaps one of his best recollections, which probably never left his thoughts, was what Jesus told him after his dreadful denials. During a breakfast several days after the Resurrection, Jesus turned to Peter and said three times, "Simon Peter do you love me?" Peter responded, "Yes, Lord you know I do." Then Jesus said, "Tend my lambs."

In other words as time and circumstance proved, Jesus was saying, "Peter, I love you, you are forgiven for what you've done, go now and minister to others." *(John 21:15-17)* Is there any wonder why Peter loved Jesus and His Word so much? Here he was down and out; eliminating himself from further service, but with a word from Jesus became completely restored and put back on track. So will it also be for you and your children, but you must read, study, and fall in love with Scripture together for this to happen. If you do then who knows what God can do with your lives, look what His words did with a young fisherman who denied Him.

Results of not Being Taught Well

If your children are not taught the Word well while growing up, they can become susceptible to just about any kind of thinking or set of beliefs, especially when they enter their teenage years. Without a solid foundation in the Word from which to draw, they could end up complacent about God, becoming more enamored with the various devices of this world, like idolizing the popular, drugs, alcohol, or material things. They may even end up rejecting Christ altogether. So if you want to minimize the possibility of poor, heart-breaking choices, then invest your time in teaching your children God's Word. *(Psalm 119:36-37)*

The Power Behind the Word

A number of years ago when I was first learning how to present the Gospel to others, the Lord really struck me on the power that stood behind and with His Word. I was on a beach in Laguna, California sharing the *Four Laws* with another college student. The *Four Laws* was a four step booklet created in the 60s by the college ministry Campus Crusade for Christ. During my days in Campus Crusade, I used it several times with good results. But during this presentation nothing worked at first, which surprised me because I was doing the best job with it that I could. As I saw this college student fading in interest, I silently prayed, saying, "Lord, what do I do next?" An inner voice responded, which I believe was the Spirit. In essence He said, "Let me take over now." So I did, and almost immediately it came to me to share what the Word had done in my own life. As I switched and began to share this, the student perked up and really began to listen. At the end when considering Christ as Savior, he said, "You know, at first

I wasn't interested in what you were saying, but then somewhere in the middle, what you began to share really hit my heart." I believe that was when the Spirit of God stepped in, changing this student's heart as only He can. I learned a lot that day about God and His Word, that all I need do is present it, and then let Him do the rest.

In respect to this, do the same with your children and just present to them what you know and let God do the rest. Is this not what He wanted the disciples to do when sending them out on their first preaching? Get away from the notion you have to be flawless in your teaching with your children, remember the power of God's Word doesn't depend on you, but on the Spirit who travels with it.

Prerequisites for Teaching

There are only three prerequisites needed to teach your children the Word; they have to do with being **faithful, available,** and **teachable.** They are what I call being **FAT** for the Lord, an acronym made up from the first letter of each of these prerequisites.

To become **faithful,** all you need to do is begin reading and studying the Word with your children, regardless of how much you know. Just "showing up" goes a long way with God. In response, He will begin to fill your mind and heart with all you need to teach them; not only for the moment but for years to come.

You need not worry about their questions, for what they will ask you at four years of age will be different than when they are 14. But even if their questions get beyond you at times, God will help for He always responds to faithfulness as Paul mentions to Timothy.

I thank Christ Jesus our Lord, who has strengthened me, because He considered me faithful, putting me into service. (I Timothy 1:12)

If for whatever reason you still feel inadequate about teaching, remember that Peter and the other disciples must have also felt the same way when asked to preach the Gospel, for they had no formal training or education. Yet, because of their **faithfulness,** God used them in a mighty way to be His teachers to the next generation of believers. He will do the same for you with your children. And just as Jesus taught all that He could while with the disciples, you should also want to do the same with your children.

He only had three-and-a-half years; you have 18 or more years.

The second prerequisite is to make yourself **available** by clearing the decks of other priorities so that you can teach your children as often as possible. This may mean rearranging your schedule, or simply dropping what you are doing to answer questions or concerns about the Word as they bring them up. Making yourself available may also mean patiently teaching your children the same lessons over and again until they grasp them. Jesus certainly did this with His disciples, who needed a great deal of re-teaching because of what they learned from their religious leaders. Because He did, they succeeded as your children will too under your instruction.

The third prerequisite is a **teachable** spirit, which is a willing attitude to learn God's truth from anyone who truly believes and follows Christ, including your own children. You might question what you could possibly learn from them; after all, they are so young and inexperienced in their faith. Yet, God may use them to teach you some of your greatest lessons if you remain teachable, for 'believing' children are filled just as much with the Holy Spirit as you. *(I Corinthians 12:6-7)* It has never been God's practice to give more of the Holy Spirit to one over another, no matter the age.

Peter is a great man to study when it comes to being teachable, particularly in respect to his talks with Paul over the Word. In their conversations he could have said, "I know more than you, after all I was with Jesus for three-and-half years and you weren't. In fact you weren't even a believer when I was with Jesus. And you definitely weren't the one to whom He said, 'The keys of the kingdom are yours.' " *(Matthew 16:18-19)*

Peter did not say these things nor was he tempted to because of his teachable and humble spirit. *(Philippians 2:3)* Thus he gave Paul his due and listened to him so that he could learn even more about God's kingdom, especially in respect to grace. His first letter brings this out when encouraging fellow believers to embrace humility.

Clothe yourselves with humility toward one another, for God is opposed to the proud, but gives grace to the humble. (I Peter 5:5)

I leave you with an illustration in my own life where being teachable paid off. Of course I would like to say I always had a teachable spirit around my kids as they grew up, but that would not be true. At least in this instance, I did set the stage for God to teach me a great lesson in parenting. It was with my son Brodie when he was ten years old. I consider this experience a Teachable Moment for me because a particular coaching hat that hung in my closet for years reminded me of what I learned that day.

At the time I was a young pastor of a fairly new church in Colorado filled with young families. In my spare time, I coached several of my son's sports. Of course, typical of me, I prepared Brodie's team as if they were competing for a high school championship with lots of practices, drills, and strategies. As a result, we won most of our games right off, but whether we won or lost, I always made sure all the boys felt good about the efforts no matter how they did, with one exception. You guessed it; my son was the only one I didn't do this with completely. If he played badly, I told him so and then went on to tell him how he could improve. If he played well, I complimented him too, but was careful not to over do it because I didn't want him to get overconfident.

Most of the time this didn't seem to rattle Brodie; he just went out and played harder the next week. Although on one particular Saturday, Brodie decided he'd had enough and spoke up. As we sat in McDonalds after the game, I began analyzing his play as I had done before when he said, "Dad, stop! Please stop!" This caught me off guard, enough so to get me to stop talking. "Listen, Dad, I love winning, and I really love the way you coach me and the team. You always seem to know what to do to win a game, and I like winning. But, Dad, there comes a time when you need to stop coaching me and just be my dad after a game." He went on to explain what being a dad meant to him, and as he talked my heart sank lower and lower, because I knew he was right. Seeing this, he switched gears, perhaps sensing what I was feeling. He said, "Now, Dad, I don't want you to stop being my coach, so let's work something out. Let's say that when I want you to stop coaching me and just be my dad, I'll tell you to take off your coach's hat. No one will know what I'm asking, just you and I."

"That's a deal, Brodie, and would you forgive me?"

"Forgiven, and forgotten Dad, just like the Lord does with our sins when we repent. Isn't that what you've always taught me?"

"Yep, it is, Brodie."

I learned a lot that day, even though it came from the lips of a ten year old. I can't credit myself for this, for the way Brodie presented himself and how the Lord moved me to be teachable made it what it turned out to be. Because of this, as well as other instances like it in the years to come, Brodie became very teachable himself, especially when we studied the

Word together.

Perhaps this is why being teachable is more essential than being a skilled communicator when it comes to teaching your children the Word. The humility that accompanies it simply is a greater ear-opener than perfect speech

Final Thoughts

As I mentioned in the beginning of chapter one, Bill Counts made a great impact on me during my college days. He taught me a great deal about God's grace, but it wasn't just his teaching that made the difference. It was the example he set of being faithful, available, and teachable, what I call being FAT.

Fat may not always be a good thing in respect to health, but it is a good thing in regard to teaching your children the Word. If you are faithful, available, and teachable (FAT) when sharing the Scripture with your children, great outcomes can happen both in the present and in the future, as my wife and I experienced also with our daughter Shannon.

Our daughter Shannon while in high school made a dinner date with Myrna and me one evening. We thought it had to do with buying her a school ring. As we sat down in a nearby Italian restaurant on a Friday evening, Shannon questioned whether we should spend so much money on the school ring that we had promised her. "After all," she said, "I would only wear it for a year or so."

Both Myrna and I agreed but were wondering where this was going? "Well, what do you have in mind Shannon?"

She quickly responded, "What about buying a purity ring for me, one that will always remind me to keep myself sexually pure until I meet my future husband one day?"

Of course Myrna and I were thrilled to hear what she had said. Almost in unison we both said, "Yes," and then talked with her about where to purchase it. After we did, she wore it with honor and commitment until she married Nic, the love of her life.

I believe one of the reasons she made such a decision on her own, was greatly due to the Word both my wife and I taught her since she was a little girl. It gave her the values to make such a decision and many more like it, as it will with your children.

Teachable Moment

As you teach your children God's Word, remember it will not only help them understand God better and assist them in making great decisions, but it will continually remind them of what God thinks of them. David stated this several times throughout his Psalms.

How precious are your thoughts toward me, O God! How vast is the sum of them! If I should count them, they would outnumber the sand...
(Psalm 139:17-18)

For this Teachable Moment take your family to a beach if possible, and if you're not near one, then pick a park with a sand pit. During your time together, ask your children to count the surrounding grains of sand. Promise them if they get the answer right, you will treat them to an ice cream cone. You may have to guide them a little as they count. Pick up some sand in your hand, for instance, and count how many grains in your hand. Then, have them guess how many hands of sand it would take to fill the area you're looking at together. Of course it could be in the millions, tens of millions, or far beyond. After they've tried for awhile, stop the count. Then tell them the Scripture teaches us that God has so many precious thoughts about us that they are more than all the grains of sand that lie before you. If for no other reason, you're going to study the Word with them so you can get just a slight glimpse of what God thinks daily of you both.

The following verses referenced in this chapter can be found in sequence on my web site, www.tmoments.com. Click on the Book Resources button located on the home page.

Luke 5:4-11; Matthew 19:27-29 27; Acts 2:14-17, 21-22, 32-33, 37-38, 40-41; Galatians 2:14-16; Acts 15:3-6, 7-11; Mark 1:14-22; Luke 9:1-2; Acts 4:13; Romans 1:15-17; Romans 3:1-2; Matthew 23:13; Matthew 9:34-35; Galatians 2:20; Romans 10:17; John 21:15-17; Psalm 119:36-37; I Corinthians 12:6-7; Matthew 16:18-19; Philippians 2:3

THREE

THE MARRIAGE CUP

(Teaching your children so they will remember)

" As for Me, this is My covenant with them," says the Lord: "My Spirit which is upon you, and My words which I have put in your mouth shall not depart from your mouth, nor from the mouth of your offspring, nor from the mouth of your offspring's offspring," says the Lord, "from now and forever."
(Isaiah 59:21)

The method you choose to teach your children is possibly one of the most important decisions you will make to help them grasp and remember the great principles of Scripture. If you don't teach them the Word in a way that is simple, clear, and memorable, then over time they will likely forget what you've taught them. That could lead them to some poor decision-making in the future because they won't know God as they should. This chapter, therefore, focuses on a method of teaching used throughout the Bible, employing illustration, analogy, comparison, parable, and even story-telling. I call these descriptive and visual ways of sharing the truth, Teachable Moments.

To establish a biblical basis, Peter and some of his letters to other Christians will be analyzed. The Trinity of the Old Testament and events like the appearance of the rainbow after the great flood will be discussed, along with Jesus' use of parables and the symbols surrounding the Last Supper. All of these examples will, hopefully, set a strong foundation for the use of Teachable Moments as a method of imparting truth.

Peter

Peter continually used vivid illustration and comparison throughout his letters to make points about the Christian life. As you might have guessed, he got his lead from Jesus, who often used them in His teachings and preaching.

One of Peter's most visual teachings came in his first letter when he shared with those he was discipling that each was an integral part of God's kingdom. He pictured them as spiritual stones making up the different parts of God's house.

You also, as living stones, are being built up as a spiritual house for a holy priesthood, to offer up spiritual sacrifices acceptable to God through Jesus Christ. (I Peter 2:5)

In addition to this illustration, Peter used many more to help his own disciples understand and remember God's truth. When talking about lifespan, he equated our bodies to grass, here today and gone tomorrow. Our so called glorious moments on earth were compared to dying and fading flowers. *(I Peter 1:24-25)* The desire to grow in the Word after coming to Christ was likened to a newborn's desire for milk. *(I Peter 2:1-2)* Jesus' role in one's faith was analogous to a building's cornerstone. *(I Peter 2:6)* Jesus' plan to stop us from running head long to destruction included placing Himself as a stumbling stone in our paths. *(I Peter 2:8)* To deal with personal pride, a picture of clothing ourselves with humility was the necessary remedy. *(I Peter 5:5)* Satan was compared to a prowling lion, seeking always to destroy us. *(I Peter 5:8)*

Peter also linked our bodies to earthly dwellings, which could only serve and last us for so many years. *(II Peter 1:12-15)* He compared those whose eyes were full of adultery, greed, arrogance, and vanity to dead springs without water. *(II Peter 2:14, 17-19)* He pictured us as dogs returning to their vomit, when returning to our old sinful lifestyles. *(II Peter 2:20-22)* And lastly, he described Christ's return like that of a thief, in that it would bring great surprise to many who would not be expecting it. *(II Peter 3:10)*

Finally, Peter was without debate one of the greatest believers to teach Christ's kingdom message to others because he believed Jesus, grasped what He taught, and lived it out in front of others. Still the way he communicated also helped to make him the great teacher he became. His use of illustrations and word pictures as evidenced above shows this. If this way of teaching helped Peter, it will certainly help you with your children. Just don't forget that as you teach them, their most memorable illustration will be how you live your life out in their presence, as it was with Peter with those he taught.

The Trinity and Jesus

The Trinity (Father, Son, and Spirit) used numerous Teachable Moments (illustrations, analogies, and comparisons) throughout the Old Testament to communicate truth. The rainbow which first appeared after the great flood was a reminder that God would never destroy the world again in such a way. *(Genesis 9:12-17)* The Tabernacle and Temple where Israel worshipped were filled with symbols and comparisons to help them remember how to conduct themselves toward God and others. For instance, the incense which daily rose from these great meeting places was a picture of prayers going up to God. A slain animal illustrated that sins were taken care of and forgiven. And the presence of the Ark was a reminder of the presence of God in one's life. *(Leviticus 4:32; Psalm 141:2; I Chronicles 28:2)*

But perhaps one of the clearest examples of a Teachable Moment in the Old Testament was delivered to the parents of Israel demonstrating God's ability to do the impossible.

Now when all the nation had finished crossing the Jordan, the Lord spoke to Joshua, saying, "Take for yourselves twelve men from the people, one man from each tribe, and command them, saying, 'Take up for yourselves twelve stones from here out of the middle of the Jordan, from the place where the priests feet are standing firm, and carry them over with you and lay them down in the lodging place where you will lodge tonight.'" (Joshua 4:1-3)

So Joshua called the twelve men whom he had appointed from the sons of Israel, one man from each tribe; and Joshua said to them, "Cross again to the ark of the Lord your God into the middle of the Jordan, and each of you take up a stone on his shoulder, according to the number of the tribes of the sons of Israel "Let this be a sign among you, so that when your children ask later, saying, 'what do these stones mean to you?'" (Joshua 4:4-6)

Now the people came up from the Jordan on the tenth of the first month and camped at Gilgal...Those twelve stones which they had taken from the Jordan, Joshua set up at Gilga. He said to the sons of Israel, "When your children ask their fathers in time to come, saying, 'what are these stones?' then you shall inform your children, saying, 'Israel crossed this Jordan on dry ground.' "For the Lord your God dried up the waters of the Jordan before you until you had crossed, just as the Lord your God had done to the Red Sea, which He dried up before us until we had crossed; that all the peoples of the earth may know that the hand of the Lord is mighty, so that you may fear the Lord your God forever." (Joshua 4:19-24)

In this Teachable Moment, the Lord used stones for Israel to remind their children of His great ability and desire to keep them safe and protected.

Years earlier, He'd saved them from the Egyptian army by splitting the Red Sea. And now He was splitting the Jordan River so they could continue their journey unhindered into the Promised Land. The stones illustratively said, "You can put your trust in Me, I will do even the impossible for you."

In the New Testament, Jesus, the second member of the Trinity, continued using similar Teachable Moments. His teachings were rich with analogies, comparisons, and parables. In fact, He seldom taught without using them in one way or another. *(John 16: 25)* The Gospels recorded over a hundred of His parables, and this doesn't even include the probability that many of these parables, along with other analogies and comparisons were taught over and over again.[1] As John pointed out at the end of his Gospel, if everything Jesus said or did was recorded, there wouldn't be enough books on earth to contain them. *(John 21:25)*

During the Last Supper Jesus used a cup of wine and a loaf of bread to remind the disciples of the great sacrifice He was going to make on the cross for them and all of mankind. *(I Peter 2:24)*

The bread symbolized the brokenness of His body during this ordeal, and the wine stood for the blood He would shed to pay for their sins. *(Luke 22:19-20)* All they needed to do in response was repent of their sins and put faith in Him. *(Mark 1:14-15)*

Jesus used the Parable of the Sower to teach about and link four types of farming soil with four types of people listening to the Gospel. *(Matthew 13:3-8, 19-23)* The teaching was an excellent Teachable Moment for the disciples because not long after they would be commissioned to present the Gospel to the world. In their travels, they would see thousands of fields like the one Jesus used in this teaching. Such would be a continual reminder of what to expect from the world, both good and bad.

A final example is Jesus' teaching to Nicodemus. In His conversation with this religious leader, He used birth as a Teachable Moment illustration to make His point about salvation. It obviously was a great illustration for Nicodemus, who later abandoned his old ways of religious thinking and accepted Christ as Lord. *(John 19:38-40)*

Now there was a man of the Pharisees, named Nicodemus, a ruler of the Jews; this man came to Jesus by night and said to Him, "Rabbi, we know that You have come from God as a teacher; for no one can do these signs that You do unless God is with him." Jesus answered and said to him, "Truly, truly, I say to you, unless one is born again he cannot see the kingdom of

God." Nicodemus said to Him, "How can a man be born when he is old? He cannot enter a second time into his mother's womb and be born, can he?" Jesus answered, "Truly, truly, I say to you, unless one is born of water and the Spirit he cannot enter into the kingdom of God That which is born of the flesh is flesh, and that which is born of the Spirit is spirit. Do not be amazed that I said to you, You must be born again." (John 3:1-7)

Parent Application

There are other reasons to use Teachable Moments as a way to teach; they are broken down under the following: *Teachable Moments Instill Concrete Thinking in Children, Teachable Moments Help Children Understand Big Words and Concepts,* and *Teachable Moments Encourage Participation and Are Simple to Do.*

Teachable Moments Instill Concrete Thinking in Children

Although there are many different types of teaching, there are two that serve as an overarching umbrella for all of them: abstract and concrete teaching. Abstract teaching focuses on the *conceptual* meaning of a subject, it is not concerned with establishing an illustration to understand or explain it. This kind of teaching best reaches cognitively mature young people and adults. It is based on supposition (premise, assumption, hypothesis), deduction (eliminating what doesn't fit), and conclusion (resulting belief). There were many abstract teachings throughout the Bible; Paul is an example of one who used them quite often. Here is an example in Romans 5.

Supposition

> *But God demonstrates His own love toward us, in that while we were yet sinners, Christ died for us. (Romans 5:8)*

Deduction

> *Much more then, having now been justified by His blood, we shall be saved from the wrath of God through Him. For if while we were enemies we were reconciled to God through the death of His Son, much more, having been reconciled, we shall be saved by His life. And not only this, but we also exult in God through our Lord Jesus Christ, through whom we have now received the reconciliation. (Romans 5:9-11)*

Conclusion

Therefore, just as through one man sin entered into the world, and death through sin, and so death spread to all men, because all sinned, for until the Law sin was in the world, but sin is not imputed when there is no law. (Romans 5:12-13)

There is nothing wrong with abstract teaching, it is biblical, but just doesn't typically reach kids when they are young. This is because they need to bridge what they have been taught with something they can see, feel, hear, or even smell in some cases. This kind of instruction is called concrete teaching, and heavily utilizes illustrations, object lessons, analogies, visual aides, and stories to make its points. And as you have seen through the Trinity in the Old Testament, Jesus in the New Testament, and Peter, this kind of instruction was used quite effectively throughout the Bible, even more so than abstract teaching.

Eventually your children will become more abstract thinkers as they grow older, but until then, concrete teaching (Teachable Moments) will speak the loudest and longest to them. So when you are teaching your children the Word, make sure an illustration goes with what you are teaching. Many times the Bible will have its own illustration, which may only require tweaking it here or there so that your kids can grasp the truth.

Teachable Moments Help Children Understand Big Words and Concepts

Another reason Teachable Moments are such an effective way to teach kids is that they help explain some pretty big words and concepts that appear in the Bible. Redemption (being purchased by God and delivered from sin's captivity), atonement (bringing man and God together), justification (making right), and sovereignty (God's control over all that happens) are just a few of these. Words like redemption and justification are easier to combine with a Teachable Moment because they are already being used within our culture in one way or another. Be cautious, though, before introducing big words of the Bible to your children: don't do too many at once, and make sure their age level can grasp the words. If in doubt, ask teachers at school or Sunday school teachers at church.

Furthermore, forgo using Teachable Moments to explain big theological words not in the Bible like Eschatological (end times) Soteriological (view of salvation), or Calvinistic (view of God's sovereignty). There's nothing wrong with these terms, but for kids and even many adults, they make complicated what was meant to be simple. Jesus did the opposite, making the complicated simple to understand.

Finally, don't be overly concerned if your children get bored or fidgety during the course of a Sunday morning sermon, it's probably because they don't understand the big words or concepts being used. Just be patient with them, and instead of chiding your children for their lack of interest, think up a Teachable Moment to share later that reflects what was taught.

Teachable Moments Encourage Participation and Are Simple to Do

The last reason why Teachable Moments are such a good way to teach is that they encourage your children's participation and are easy to do. When doing a Teachable Moment, the illustration, analogy, or story you choose will spark a great deal of discussion. Your children will likely have a lot of questions about the Teachable Moment and how it links up with what you wanted to teach. They may even want to add to it or do a totally different one. But regardless of their response, the point is they are actively engaged and participating, rather than passively sitting and listening.

Teachable Moments are easy to do in most cases, and much less difficult than explaining abstract truth. They are easy because you don't have to qualify as a professional Bible teacher to do them. Peter certainly wasn't a professional when he started teaching, he didn't have any academic or rhetorical training; he was only a fisherman willing to learn. Because of this willingness, God used him in a mighty way to teach others, as He will with you and your children. *(Acts 4: 13)*

To get started, all you need do is read a portion of God's Word with your children, and then come up with a memorable illustration, symbol, analogy, comparison, or story to represent what you've learned.

Final Thoughts

If you are still unsure how to get started using Teachable Moments with your children, then after reading this book, begin with the 24 Teachable Moments listed in its companion book, *Sowing Teachable Moments Year One.* These teachings should take you about a year to complete if you do one every other week. After you're finished, go to the ones included on my web site. I currently have over one hundred from which to choose. I can assure you that if you go through all of these, you will have no trouble developing Teachable Moments on your own with your children for years to come.

Teachable Moment

The following Teachable Moment comes from an article I wrote one Easter. It highlights Jesus' use of a cup of wine to teach and remind believers in every generation of the sacrifice He made on the cross. This is a teaching your family will hear over and over again as you take communion together. It also reminds you to teach your children in like manner with memorable symbols, illustrations, analogies, comparisons, or stories.

Will You Marry Me?

"Let us be glad and rejoice, and give honor to Him, for the marriage of the Christ (Lamb) is come, and his wife has made herself ready." (Revelation 19:7)

The Last Supper occurred midway between Palm Sunday and the Resurrection. At this time, Jesus gathered His disciples to celebrate the Passover feast. During this traditional dinner, He shared with them about His coming sacrifice and the New Covenant, which had never been taught before. His message was so profound and memorable that Christians still recite and repeat it over and over today in every part of the world.

The four accounts of Matthew 26:26-28, Mark 14:22-26, Luke 22:14-20 and I Corinthians 11:23-26 record the Last Supper, each add different detail. So that you can see the entire account, I've merged these four passages together, paraphrasing where needed. I have also included the background and meaning of the four cups of wine Jesus presented during the Last Supper. These cups were an integral part of a Passover Dinner, particularly the third one.

The Last Supper

During the night which Jesus was betrayed, He sat down with the disciples for dinner and told them He desired greatly to eat the Passover feast with them before He was to suffer. Jesus then said, "I won't eat it again like this until the kingdom is fulfilled."

He then passed out the first cup of wine which was called the Kiddush. This cup started things off, consecrating the entire evening to God. A second cup was soon offered representing a blessing, similar to what we would offer to God before a meal.

While the disciples were eating, Jesus took bread, gave thanks, broke it, and gave it to them saying, "This is my body which is given for you, take and eat in remembrance of me."

Then Jesus offered the third cup of wine, which was called the cup of redemption, salvation, or grace. It was the most significant cup because it represented being forgiven and united with God. When Jesus offered this cup, He gave thanks, and passed it to the disciples saying, "This cup which is poured out for you is the New Covenant in My blood. Drink it in remembrance of Me." Afterward He said, "I will not drink from it anew with you until My Father's kingdom comes. And as often as you eat this bread and drink this cup, remember you proclaim My death until I return."

Lastly, He followed up with a fourth cup; it was called the cup of benediction, ending the dinner and their time together. As they all got up to leave, they sang a Hymn to conclude their time together.

Although all four cups were important and had their symbolic meanings, it was the third that was the most significant. Not only because of what it meant, but because of what Jesus said after offering it to the disciples. This cup at Passover was called the cup of redemption, salvation, or grace, and was to be a reminder of God's continuing desire to forgive man and return him to His presence. All anyone had to do was repent and believe.

After giving out this third cup at the Last Supper, Jesus spoke of a New Covenant, a forever contract between God and man that took effect after the cross. Ray Vander Laan, a noted Bible teacher who authored the video series, "That the World May Know" illustrates the meaning of the New Covenant very well, particularly in respect to taking communion.[2] He compares the New Covenant of which Jesus spoke with the typical new covenant agreement young Jewish couples in love had to procure if they wanted to marry.

The engagement and marriage process wasn't easy for young Jewish couples; it required a great deal of patience. The whole process began with the couple expressing their desire to marry with each of their own families, the boy with his, and the girl with hers. If all went well, the father of the young man set up a meeting with the girl's father at her house. On the day of the meeting, the young man and his father went to the girl's home to meet with her father. The girl was not a part of the meeting, but sat in a room nearby, most likely with her mother. As the three men gathered, only the fathers talked. Conversations varied from family to family, but at the end of their talk, a bride price had to be agreed upon between the fathers.

This didn't mean the girl was being sold, but because of the girl's value to her own family, compensation for such a loss was needed and required. That price in some cases could be as high as the cost of a new home. I remember when giving this message at my own daughter's wedding before communion; I looked at Shannon and said before all, "You are worth a city of homes to our family." And she was!

After the agreement was struck, the men took a cup of wine and drank from it to seal the deal. The young man's father then gave the cup to his son to take to his bride-to-be. The cup was called the Covenant or New Covenant cup. Upon finding her, he needed to say nothing, for the cup said everything. When lifting it up and offering it to her, he was saying, "I love you, the price has been paid, I will give my life for you, and will you marry me?" The girl needed to say nothing either, for if she took the cup and drank from it, she was saying, "I love you; I accept your offer of marriage; I will be faithful to you all the days of my life."[3]

And so when Jesus raised the third cup and said to His disciples, "This cup which is poured out for you is the New Covenant in My blood," was He not saying, "I love you; the price has been paid; will you be my bride; will you marry me?" And when you respond at your next communion as you drink from the cup, just as the disciples did, are you not saying, "I do love you Lord; I accept your offer of marriage; and I will be faithful to you all the days of my life." I pray so.

Finally, should you want to go a step further and share this Teachable Moment with your children, begin by reading or explaining what is in this article. If possible, and only you can be the judge of this, compare how your engagement and marriage compared to the young Jewish couple in the illustration. Compare other things too, like your marriage proposal to the cup of wine offered to the young girl or your marriage certificate to Jesus' New Covenant.

Then, the next time your family takes communion together, see what your children remember about communion; I'll bet they will remember a lot!

The following verses referenced in this chapter can be found in sequence on my web site, www.tmoments.com. Click on the Book Resources button located on the home page.

I Peter 1:24-25; I Peter 2:1-2; I Peter 2: 6; I Peter 2: 8; I Peter 5:5; I Peter 5:8; II Peter 1:12-15 ; II Peter 2:14,17-19; II Peter 2:20-22; II Peter 3:10; Genesis 9:12-17; Leviticus 4:32 Psalm 141: 2; I Chronicles 28:2; John 16:25; John 21:25; I Peter 2:24; Luke 22: 19-20; Mark 1:14-15; Matthew 13:3-8; 18-23; John 19:38-40; Acts 4:13; Matthew 26: 26-28; Mark 14:22-26; Luke 22:14-20; I Corinthians 11:23-26

SECTION II

The I in TIPS for Parenting

(The importance of building intimate relationships with your children)

"I am the good shepherd, and I know My own and My own know Me."
John 10:14

This section is based on **321** verses in **127** different passages of Scripture.

Thoughts ahead

If you find in your schedule that you are too busy to regularly spend quality time with your children, teaching them life's lessons through the Word, then you are simply too busy. Chapter 5

If your children only see the victories or the stellar parts of your Christian life and character, then they will end up only seeing one part of who you are. Instead they need to see all of you, even the frustrations, failures, and sins that make up your life. Chapter 6

The primary goal of discipline is not to punish your children for every wrong or foolish deed, but to create within them a heart that wants to do right. Chapter 9

FOUR

GARY

(Building intimacy with your children)

When I was a son to my father, tender and the only son in the sight of my mother, then He taught me and said to me, let your heart hold fast my words; keep My commandments and live; Acquire wisdom! Acquire understanding!
(Proverbs 4:3-5)

The following section is the second key in discipling your children through Teachable Moments. It is titled Intimacy; which is the I in the acronym TIPS *(Teaching, Intimacy, Preparation, Sowing)*. It is identified so because it best expresses the kind of relationship you need to have with your children, one that embodies love, closeness, friendship, and a deep bond.

Without intimacy, teaching your children the Scriptures would likely become a fruitless effort. For them to listen and learn from you, they need to know you really care, and that you truly want to be with them.

Before outlining what is ahead, let me first share with you a heart-warming story where many of the components of intimacy were present and experienced. I call this Gary's story, but really it is a story of many young people whom became wonderfully intimate with the Lord and each other.

Gary's Story

I met Gary and many other young people during my first youth ministry at Hillcrest Church in 1971. Even though I had worked with young people for years, this was my first full-time ministry position. I accepted this position in late August, which came just in time for me, because I was engaged to be married in December and needed a job. Both Myrna (my fiancée) and I were in Los Angeles at the time where she was in her last semester at UCLA.

Upon arriving in Seattle, I was amazed how beautiful the Northwest was and how unpopulated by comparison to California. Los Angeles had always been my home, while Myrna's had been on the Central California coast. When I reached my destination in my small U-Haul truck, I met some great kids who were very willing to help me move into my house. Reverend

Brown, the senior pastor, was also very accommodating, making me feel right at home.

In my initial days of ministry, I tried taking things slowly, making every effort to see the dynamics of the youth group I inherited. For the first month or so, I just observed, did a few socials with them, and some teaching in the high school department on Sunday mornings. By the middle of October, I realized I really had to do much more than this, as many of the kids who came on Sunday mornings either didn't know the Lord or were not much interested in Him. Some, for example, came to the youth group meetings merely for the parties and sporting events, while others only showed up on Sundays because their parents forced them to be there. An elder who greatly helped me during those early days called these kids the *frozen chosen*, because they were ice cold toward God yet in church every Sunday.

One of my first ministry moves was to meet with the high school kids on Wednesday nights rather than Sunday mornings. I did so because I felt that on a week night I would have more time to spend with each of them, an important component of intimacy that will be discussed later. I surmised that only those interested in spiritual growth would come on Wednesday nights, which is exactly what happened. It was a bit of a risk, as I sensed a lot of church parents might not like their kids going to another youth meeting. After all, Sunday mornings was enough.

In respect to my Sunday morning duties, I didn't abandon them; I turned the *frozen chosen* over to a very popular school counselor who attended the church and was a good teacher. Then I switched my Sunday morning teaching duties to the college group also under my care. This ended up working well for me because the college group was very open to following the Lord with their lives. When I taught, they were engaged, and when I asked for help on Wednesday nights, many set aside their studies and social life to help.

As October moved into November, Wednesday nights began to pick up steam. The high school and college students who came began inviting their friends, who invited their friends, who invited their friends. Week after week brought more kids and greater enthusiasm, as those who came were being met with and taught the Scripture one-on-one, which is a key to discipleship and a component of intimacy. After Myrna joined me in December things really began to pick up, because I had someone who could meet with all the girls. Eventually, there was no better spot to be on Wednesday nights than at Andrew's Place (the name we gave our meeting room in the basement of the church). In the midst of the growth, I tried staying true to my goal of meeting personally with each individual, but this became harder as time went on.

I started another meeting on Sunday nights to give more time to the kids involved. We held it at my house and called it our *Body Life* meetings. The name was taken from Ray Stedman's book, *Body Life*, in which he focused on building relationships within the body of Christ, the church.[1] Our *Body Life* meetings started out with a variety of contemporary and traditional Christian songs which set the atmosphere for most evenings. Kids were encouraged to openly share their lives with each other after each song. As they did, several spontaneously prayed and offered advice and help.

One meeting built upon the next until these young people grew incredibly open and transparent with each other, another important component of building intimacy with your children. They shared their joys, hurts, achievements, failures, hopes, discouragements, victories, and even their own personal sins. This helped me greatly. I was able to step back from doing all of the discipling and intimacy-building as they began doing much of it themselves. They also began teaching the Word to one another, as quickly as they learned it.

As we entered the second year, this newly birthed youth group began to love each other with an Agape type of love, the third great component in building intimacy. Agape is a Greek term which is used for love throughout the original texts of the Bible to describe God's love for all of His creation.[2] It is two pronged in that it accepts us where we are through His grace, mercy, and forgiveness, yet challenges us to be all we should be through discipline, reproof, and correction.

As the years passed our youth group grew in their influence at school, witnessing to many and bringing several to Christ. In addition to sharing what Christ was doing in their lives, they humbly served their friends in many loving ways. Time and again they came to their school friend's aid, whether it was helping them on a school project or more importantly getting through a difficult circumstance at school or home.

Needless to say, Myrna and I were greatly inspired by this group of kids, especially in regard to the intimacy we experienced with them. In the years to come, we tried to apply the same kind of intimacy with our own children. Our only sadness in all of this was that we eventually had to leave the youth group when God called us to another ministry. We never stopped loving these kids, nor did we stop keeping in contact with many of them for over forty years. That's one of the great results of true intimacy; the kind you want to have with your children.

Many of these young people continued well in their faith becoming wonderful Christian parents, church elders, Sunday school workers, pastors, wives of pastors, youth ministers, missionaries, great church layman and even noted speakers for the kingdom.

I want to make special mention of one in the group, a guy named Gary. I do so because his story brings out the one component of intimacy not mentioned so far, that of encouragement. Gary first started coming to Wednesday nights when he was 16, and he came only because he wanted to play basketball for our church team. I coached the team and made it a requirement for all boys outside of the church to come on Wednesday nights. Gary was one of those. He wasn't too excited about coming to church, especially in the middle of the week, but he loved basketball and was willing to make the sacrifice. As the months passed, his interest in Christ became more and more evident, until he finally made a decision to accept Him as Lord and Savior. The change in Gary was dramatic, so much so that others at school started coming to Wednesday nights. And if that wasn't enough, he worked tirelessly to help the youth group in every way he could. He was often the first to show up and the last to leave at almost every gathering and was a constant source of encouragement to everyone.

After Myrna and I left for our next ministry in California, we kept in close contact with Gary. Even though he was very young, he ended up to be one of the most encouraging friends we ever had. A year after we moved, something happened to Gary that devastated him and us. He was diagnosed with an unusual cancer that didn't offer him a lot of hope. Of course, when Myrna and I found out we were very concerned and immediately began praying and calling him, but it only worsened. After a number of months, I decided to fly up to Seattle to encourage Gary. Myrna couldn't come because she had just had our first baby.

During my short time with Gary, I recalled with him the great days we had together in the youth group, what might possibly be the Lord's will in the days ahead, and then we looked at Scriptures that offered hope. I didn't mince words with Gary about the days ahead; he would have it no other way, for the Lord was either going to heal him or take him. Gary was content with either one, but I wasn't.

Right before I was getting ready to return to California, the Spirit hit me with the idea to hold one last *Body Life* meeting with the old youth group, like the ones we used to have at my house. I made a few calls to some of the other kids, located a home in which to meet, and wondered how many might come. Far more than I expected, as it turned out, just like the old days. As we began to sing and pray, the attention of course turned toward Gary and his cancer. But before leading in prayer for him, I asked each to give a reason why they felt God should heal him. I went on to explain that God does listen to us, and that even though He may have good reason to take Gary, He may also have good reason not to. What we needed to do was present the Lord with a case for his staying. And we did, for over an hour or so, everyone openly made their case to God, explaining why Gary should live out a full life on earth. To say that this time was encouraging to Gary is an understatement, for it brought life to his spirit, as well as to his broken down six foot, 135 pound body.

As the meeting came to an end, we all laid hands on Gary and asked the Lord to heal him. It was a great note to end on, because everyone showed how much they cared. Expressing care and concern is the foundation of all encouragement, a component of intimacy you must always apply with your children.

The next morning I flew out, and when I got home I told Myrna everything, giving special attention to what went on in our *Body Life* meeting. She was so heartened by it, wishing she could have been there too. Then almost as soon as I finished telling her, the phone rang and it was Gary. He excitedly thanked me for the time I spent with him, the prayers, the uplifting words, and of course the *Body Life* meeting arranged for him. He then abruptly switched gears (as is typical of Gary) telling me he had just been to the doctor's office to check on the advancement of his cancer. So I said, "What'd he say, Gary; how'd it go?" "Well it's gone; there is no trace of the cancer, whatsoever." I was shocked at first but happily so. Gary went on and told me how baffled the doctors were, that they couldn't explain how such a cancer could just go away. In fact, from their experience, the cancer just could not disappear as it did. In the midst of their quandary on what to write in their medical report, Gary told them it was a miracle from God and that this is what they needed to put down on the report.

A year later Gary called again, but this time he asked me to come up to Seattle to perform his wedding to Tina, a girl who had encouraged him throughout his whole ordeal. And of course I did, taking Myrna along with me this time. As the wedding started, I walked out with Gary but could not resist saying to him first, "You know, Gary, I was planning on doing your funeral about this time last year not your wedding." Gary looked at me with a rather victorious smile and said, "I guess God had a better plan."

What's Ahead?

In the above story, there were four components of intimacy which will be further explored in the next six chapters. Each plays an important role when discipling and teaching your children the Scriptures. All four come from God's Word and fall under the following: *Time, Transparency, Encouragement,* and *Agape Love.*

Please take special note that this section on Intimacy is broken up into two parts, the first dealing with the importance of spending time with your children, the value of teaching them openness and transparency, and the necessity of encouragement (Chapters 5-7). The second part deals with Agape love (Chapters 8-10) and another personal story which brings to life the importance of using discipline with your children, as well as grace, mercy, and forgiveness.

The Biblical Examples

To exemplify a close and intimate relationship with your children, David and Jesus will be the primary biblical figures used as examples in this section. David was chosen for several different reasons, none of which have to do with his parenting, as sadly, he wasn't a very good father. *(II Samuel 13:8, 11-15 20-23, 28-31, 34, 39; II Samuel 14:24 28-29; II Samuel 15: 13-14; 2 Samuel 18:14, 33)* Regardless, he had a great heart for God, was a very good king, and had a lot to say in his Psalms about intimacy, particularly Psalm 23, which will be cited and referenced in each succeeding chapter of this section. Jesus and His intimate relationship with the disciples will also be explored. From both David and Jesus, along with many other Scriptural accounts, there are plenty of biblical guidelines to follow as you build the kind of intimacy with your children that will draw them closer to God and His Word.

Final Thoughts

This whole account of the youth group and Gary brings back great memories of the close-knit and intimate relationships we had with each other. Many of these kids later on became parents themselves and developed similar relationships with their own children. Some had more success than others, because sometimes parents can do everything right, but their kids still may not end up as hoped. Look at God in this respect; He did everything possible to save and develop close relationships with everyone He created. *(John 3:16; 2 Peter 3:9)* Yet, as we all know today, because of the evil in our world, not all of God's creation turned out as He had wished. This is because along with everything He did for His creation, He also gave everyone freedom to choose from birth, to comply or not, to say yes or no. So it will be with your children too, and like God, you must do everything you can to help them make the right choices, which begins with building an intimate relationship and teaching them the Word.

One last note in regard to Gary, his doctors rankled for years to determine just what he had: cancer, blood virus, crone's disease, or something else. And even though they are still not completely sure of what it was, there was no doubt that when he showed up after our *Body Life* meeting something medically phenomenal had happened. As one doctor simply put it then, "It's a miracle, no doubt about it, no other explanation, none."

The following verses referenced in this chapter can be found in sequence on my web site, www.tmoments.com. Click on the Book Resources button located on the home page.

II Samuel 13:8, 11-15 20-23, 28-31, 34, 39; II Samuel 14:24 28-29; II Samuel 15:13-14; II Samuel 18:14, 33; John 3:16; II Peter 3:9

FIVE

DEVELOPING GREAT DECISION MAKERS

(Spending time with your children)

He leads me in the paths of righteousness. . .
(Psalm 23:3)

The first component to establish an intimate and close relationship with your children is to spend time with them. If you do, they will likely listen to you, whether it's from the Word or anything else you want to teach them. Spending time with them says that you have made them an important priority in your life. This often melts their hearts and opens their ears, as it does with any of us regardless of age or station in life. Think about it; when people give you their time, don't you feel closer to them and listen more intently to what they have to say? Of course you do, because it opens the door for greater love, closeness, friendship, and bonds with one another and these are the main tenets of intimacy.

For that reason, spending time with your children is important, especially if you want to build a deep and lasting relationship with them. It was certainly important to David and Jesus whom we will look at first for perspective and guidelines to follow.

David

David wrote scores of Psalms during the course of his life, but perhaps the greatest was Psalm 23 which described his intimate relationship with the Lord. In this Psalm, David used his experience as a shepherd to describe God's love relationship with him as his shepherd.

The part of David's Psalm 23 that refers to the importance of spending time together, an essential in building intimacy with your children, comes from verse three, "*...He leads me in the paths of righteousness for His name sake.*" At first glance, this idea may be hard to see in this verse, but if you look closely at David's life as a shepherd, you will catch sight of it.

David, like all good shepherds of his day, led his sheep on one path after another in search of new grass to eat and water to drink. During these long treks, which usually took place during the summers, David spent countless hours getting to know his sheep and letting them get to know him.[1] Often they were together during these months, 24 hours a day, seven days a week. Like most shepherds who loved their flocks, David slept standing up with a rod in one hand and a staff in the other; a presence that not only gave a secure feeling to his sheep, but also scared off many would-be predators or thieves.[2,3,4] Because of the time David spent with his flock on these paths, his sheep listened to him and followed his guidance. Just as your children will if you give them your time.

So when David wrote, *"He guides me in the paths of righteousness for His name sake,"* the paths for David meant God was with him day in and day out, helping him make right decisions. Some of those right decisions later included facing Goliath with faith and a sling and waiting on God to do His work with Saul before taking over the throne.

Jesus

Unlike David, Jesus was not a shepherd in his early years, but rather a carpenter. Yet, He is known as the Good Shepherd because of the way He loved, cared for, and gave of His time to others. *(John 10:10-14)* It is amazing that with all the demands made on Jesus' time by so many, He opted to give a majority of it to just a few disciples. Like David when he was a young shepherd boy, Jesus spent hours with His flock of disciples, teaching them what they needed to know to handle life and carry on after He was gone.

For approximately three-and-a-half years he spent day and night with them. When you break this down, it works out to about a 1000 days, or 12 to 15 thousand hours. During these days and hours, He developed a personal relationship with each of His disciples that was intimate and family-like. The time Jesus spent leading them from one faith experience to the next was not only the key to their spiritual development, but was an essential component to spreading the Gospel to the entire world. Through them other disciples where made and churches begun, resulting in hundreds of millions of believers over the centuries. All of this resulted because Jesus took time to get to know, mature, and equip a few disciples with the tools to handle life and do ministry. If you think of all the ways Jesus could have reached the world during His most productive years on earth, spending quality time with just a few is not an option most people would consider.

Even when the crowds grew to great numbers, Jesus walked away after ministering to spend time with His disciples. *(Matthew 13:36; Matthew*

20:17; Mark 3:7-10; Mark 4:33-34; Luke 10:23) No matter what, He never put the disciples on the backburner in regard to His time, not even in His most popular moments.

If Jesus spent so much time with His disciples, developing an intimate relationship with them, not rushing any phase of their spiritual development, then you should do the same with your children. If you do, imagine what impact and difference you or they will make in this world, certainly much more than if you don't.

Parent Application

In looking at some parenting applications in regard to the time you need to devote to your children, there are a few perspectives and guidelines to consider. They are listed under the following titles: *Spending Time Helps You Know Your Children, Too Busy Is Too Busy, Children Are Worth Your Time,* and *Making Time Can Have Different Venues.*

Spending Time Helps You Know Your Children

Spending time with your children not only helps to build a close and intimate relationship with them, it also aids in understanding their personality and what inspires them. This is what David experienced with his sheep on those long treks together through the mountains. He learned first hand which sheep needed to be pushed and which didn't, which ones could lead and which couldn't. The more time he spent, the better he got to know how to shepherd each of them. The same will be true of you; the more time you spend with your children, the better you'll become in raising and discipling them for the Lord. Correspondingly, they also will learn how to understand you, which will help them to respond to your guidance and leadership.

Our children, Brodie and Shannon, were very different from one another and quite different from Myrna and me. As we studied the Bible together, one liked to debate whereas the other just wanted answers. In sports one was aggressive, the other more laid back. In school one loved the politics of it, running for every office possible, and the other didn't. In academics one had it easy and the other had to work hard for everything. By spending time with both of them as Myrna and I did, it helped us understand who they were, which led to a deeper and closer relationship. The same can be true for you if you just give your kids the time they need and get to deeply know them.

Too Busy Is Too Busy

If you find in your schedule that you are too busy to regularly spend quality time with your children, teaching them life's lessons through the Word, then you are simply too busy. Simple as that! Busyness usually comes from having too many priorities in your life, more than what God wants you to have. Jesus set the example in this respect as He could have spent His entire time on earth speaking and ministering to the multitudes. Think of the crowds He could have drawn week after week had He not spent so much time with the disciples. He decided against this because His small group of disciples was more important to Him; they were His priority as your children should be in your life.

One of the ways to determine if you are too busy is to note where and what you are doing with your time. If your time is mostly consumed by interests such as work, education, self-betterment pursuits, various pleasures, hobbies, and social activities outside the home, then you are probably not giving your children the time they need. God gave you children for several reasons, and one is to spend as much time with them as possible. No matter what time demands or constraints you are under, your children and spouse need to be your priority. They are the ones needing most of your time, as was true of Jesus and His disciples.

For this to happen you may have to make some changes in your life. If so, here are a few suggestions to get started. First, pray for wisdom to make your family the priority. Jesus told His disciples that if they wanted anything they should just ask; so ask Him! *(Matthew 7:7-11)* Second, seek out advice from other successful Christian parents. It is likely they have had the same challenge at one time. Third, proclaim openly to your family and others what you are trying to do. It is one thing to make a silent commitment to make a change, but quite another to declare it before others. If you keep it to yourself, then you can fizzle out on your commitment without anybody knowing, except God of course. But if you let others know, especially those in your family, then you are much more likely to follow through, because they will help you keep your commitment. The fourth suggestion is to consider downsizing what you want to live on. Now, I didn't say what you "need", but what you "want" to live on. Consider moving to a home or apartment that is more affordable, one that doesn't require you to work extra hours or your spouse to work to make the mortgage or monthly rent. If you can, consider changing your job for another if it's taking you away from your family too often. If you can do none of these for the present, then cut your expenses. Ask yourself if you need that new car, furniture, computer, or big screen TV. Remember, the more you buy, the more you will have to earn to pay for it, which means less time with your family.

Last, give time to your children because they're important. With the exception of your spouse, the relationship with your children is perhaps the most important of all relationships. The disciples were important to Jesus, enough so that He spent most of His ministry time with them. You should do no less with your family if you really want to build lasting intimacy with them.

Children Are Worth Your Time

Children are worth your time as there will come a day when they will be the ones holding your family together and doing God's bidding to reach the next generation for Him. Although Jesus spent most of His ministry years with the disciples, giving children time was very important to Him. He made this very clear one day with the disciples when they tried to shoo off some children who had been brought to Him. They concluded these children weren't important enough to take up His time. Before they whisked them away, Jesus stopped the disciples. He then took the little ones to Himself and held them in His arms, blessing each one. Afterward He taught the disciples, as well as the parents listening that day, about the importance and priority of children. *(Matthew 19: 13-15; Luke 18: 15-17)* If Jesus thought so highly of children, can you think any less of yours?

And they were bringing children to Him so that He might touch them; but the disciples rebuked them. But when Jesus saw this, He was indignant and said to them, "Permit the children to come to Me; do not hinder them; for the kingdom of God belongs to such as these. Truly I say to you, whoever does not receive the kingdom of God like a child will not enter it at all." And He took them in His arms and began blessing them, laying His hands on them. (Mark 10:13-16)

Making Time Can Have Different Venues

Making time for your children so that they can learn God's truth can be accomplished in many different ways and venues. You don't have to be their Sunday school teacher or Awana leader to do so. It can mean just being with them during their various interests, hobbies, school functions, or other activities. As indicated earlier, I spent a lot of time coaching my kids in their sports. The time we spent together bonded us, as well as giving us many illustrations and material for our Bible studies. Some of those lessons were about winning and losing with grace, being a good teammate, doing your best, recognizing what's important, and responding to the foul-mouthed and the braggart. However the whole point of this was not the life lessons we learned, but the life and intimacy we built doing it together. Start by giving time to your children, this helps create intimacy with them, and then find out what they love or do best. Finally, create some kind of teaching ministry or sharing opportunity around it. They will love it, and they will love you for doing it.

Final Thoughts

As portrayed in the opening story with Gary, I spent a lot of time with him. If I hadn't, then our relationship would never have been as warm or close as it turned out to be. Without that relationship, I don't think Gary would have listened to me very long as I taught the Scriptures, no matter how well I presented it. I believe the same is true with parents and their children. If parents don't spend time building a relationship with their children, they will likely not attend themselves to the Word, no matter how much they are taken to church. Don't take the chance; spend time with your children so they will not only love you all the more but God and His Word to the fullest.

Teachable Moment

In our home both my wife and I spent about 30 minutes before bedtime each night listening to our children's thoughts, praying with them, and singing some of their favorite Christian songs. At the end, I often shared a passage of Scripture or devotional. We did this most nights during their early years. A routine they really liked, looked forward to, and called "night, nights." Later, when they were older, we switched to morning devotions as we rode to school together.

If this is something you are interested in doing, I encourage you to try it, for it really helped us grow closer as a family and to the Lord. It also gave us a great foundation in the Scripture. Before you get started, though, I suggest a visual reminder to help you be as consistent as you can, because in all honesty, as the years rolled by, sometimes we forgot to do our family devotions for days at a time.

One suggestion is to create a big poster or paper clock you make together with your children to hang in one of their rooms. Make sure the hands on the clock point to the time of your devotion. Give the clock a name, perhaps something from the Bible expressing your time together around the Word. You could call it the devotional clock for example. Let your children help choose the name; kids love naming things because it makes it special when they do. And of course, you want every part of your devotional time together including the clock or poster to be special.

God speed, I hope you have as good an experience as we had as a family.

The following verses referenced in this chapter can be found in sequence on my web site, www.tmoments.com. Click on the Book Resources button located on the home page.

John 10:10-14; Matthew 13:36; Matthew 20:17; Mark3:7-10; Mark 4:33-34; Luke 10:43; Matthew 7: 7-11; Matthew 19:13-15; Luke 18:15-17

SIX

SPGS

(Pronounced SPAHGS)

(Teaching your children openness and transparency)

He restores my soul;...You have anointed my head with oil.
(Psalm 23:3,5)

The second component to establishing intimacy with your children is to teach them how to be open and transparent with you and others. This comes not only from what you share with them in the Scripture, but also how you model openness and transparency.

A movie came out a number of years ago called the *Lake House* with Keanu Reeves and Sandra Bullock. I liked the movie because it had a good story line, but what made it unique was the setting of a house made of glass. I don't think I had ever seen one like it. As you looked at the house from the outside, there wasn't anything that couldn't be seen on the inside with the exclusion of bathrooms and dressing areas. Those rooms obviously needed privacy as do some areas in your Christian life. I mention this glass house because it is a good picture of the openness and transparency God wants you to have with your children as you build a relationship with them; one that all Christians should pursue with one another.

The Scriptures are full of examples of God's people being open and transparent; David was no exception as you will see in his Psalm 23 and several other Psalms he wrote. In respect to the Lord, the comments Jesus made without reservation to others will be reviewed, particularly those expressing His love, joy, anger, grief, sadness, disappointment, and even disgust.

David

When David wrote in Psalm 23, verses three and five, "*He restores my soul and anoints my head with oil,*" he was talking about God's restoring and healing work in his life. Also indicated in these verses is an indirect teaching about openness and transparency, another key ingredient to David's intimate relation with God.

As a shepherd, it was David's responsibility to get his flock from one pasture to the next for new grass to eat and water to drink. He had to plan each trek well, because sheep by nature don't have much stamina or good sense. If the journey was too long they would simply quit and give up, even if it meant perishing. In their state of tiredness they didn't hesitate to let David know of their feelings, whether it was by lying down, going off another direction, or letting out a discouraged or disgruntled *bah* (a sheep's cry). When they got to a new pasture and stream of water, they also expressed themselves by a contented look and a relaxed *bah*.

Sheep also expressed themselves when hurt, immediately seeking David's help. In most cases he used olive oil to sooth their wounds.[1] At other times, especially when he found them banging their heads against the rocks, he would pour oil into their nostrils. He anointed their nostrils because it was quite common for flies to lay eggs there, and if oil was not applied, then the newly hatched flies eventually worked their way to the sheep's brain, driving them crazy and causing death.[2]

A sheep's openness and transparency was therefore vital in getting help for their various needs and hurts. David saw himself in the same way with God, his shepherd. When he was needy and desirous of restoration, he expressed it openly to God and others as his sheep had done with him. When hurt either physically or emotionally, he also let it be known, hardly ever keeping any of his feelings from God or others. Sometimes he was hurt because of what he had done wrong, at other times because he was a victim of another's actions. *(Psalm 38:1-8; Psalm 139:5)* David came forth with his feelings before God and others, which was a great mark of his maturity and perhaps why God used him as much as He did.

The following are some comments David made about himself, some are complimentary, and some are not. As you will see he was not afraid to share just about anything, which hopefully will be true of you and your children one day.

David's open acknowledgement of his failures and sins

Then David said to Nathan, "I have sinned against the Lord."… (II Samuel 12:13)

Be gracious to me, O God, according to Your lovingkindness; according to the greatness of Your compassion blot out my transgressions. Wash me thoroughly from my iniquity and cleanse me from my sin. For I know my transgressions, and my sin is ever before me. Against You, You only, I have sinned and done what is evil in Your sight, So that You are justified when You speak and blameless when You judge." (Psalm 51:1-4)

David's transparent expression of joy

Now it was told King David, saying, the Lord has blessed the house of Obed-edom and all that belongs to him, on account of the ark of God. David went and brought up the ark of God from the house of Obed-edom into the city of David with gladness. And David was dancing before the Lord with all his might, and David was wearing a linen ephod. (II Samuel 6:12 & 14)

David's candid admission of disappointment with himself

But I am a worm and not a man, a reproach of men and despised by the people. All who see me sneer at me... (Psalm 22:6-7)

David's unconcealed confession of defeat

I am poured out like water, and all my bones are out of joint; my heart is like wax; it is melted within me. My strength is dried up like a potsherd, and my tongue cleaves to my jaws; and You lay me in the dust of death. For dogs have surrounded me; a band of evildoers has encompassed me; they pierced my hands and my feet. I can count all my bones... (Psalm 22:14-17)

David's unashamed dependence on God

The Lord is my rock and my fortress and my deliverer, my God, my rock, in whom I take refuge; my shield and the horn of my salvation, my stronghold. (Psalm 18:2)

David's uninhibited disclosure of the surrounding pressures:

Give ear to my prayer, O God; and do not hide Yourself from my supplication. Give heed to me and answer me; I am restless in my complaint and am surely distracted, because of the voice of the enemy, because of the pressure of the wicked; for they bring down trouble upon me and in anger they bear a grudge against me. (Psalm 55:1-3)

David's pronounced praise for God

My heart is steadfast, O God; I will sing, I will sing praises, even with my soul. Awake, harp and lyre; I will awaken the dawn! I will give thanks to You, O Lord, among the peoples, and I will sing praises to You among the nations. For Your lovingkindness is great above the heavens. (Psalm 108:1-3)

David's honest declaration of his fears

I sought the Lord, and He answered me, and delivered me from all my fears. (Psalm 34:4)

David's unreserved love for God

"I love You, O Lord, my strength." (Psalm 18:1)

Jesus

David was a good model of transparency, but Jesus was the perfect model of openness. He displayed His feelings not only before the disciples but also with the crowds who came to see and hear Him. Some of the positive feelings and emotions He openly displayed included love, joy, rejoicing and happiness. On the opposite end of the spectrum He displayed anger, grief, distress, sadness, disappointment, and disgust. Evidence for each of these positive and negative feelings and emotions turn up in the following passages.

Love

Jesus was open about His love for the disciples and others as well. He said, "I love you," in so many ways. During a teaching on the Vinedresser in the Gospel of John, He said, *"Just as the Father has loved Me, I have also loved you..." (John 15:9)* Another was the feelings He expressed to the Rich Young Ruler in the Gospel of Mark.

And he (Rich Young Ruler) said to Him, "Teacher, I have kept all these things from my youth up." Looking at him, Jesus felt a love for him and said to him, "One thing you lack: go and sell all you possess and give to the poor, and you will have treasure in heaven; and come, follow Me." (Mark 10:20-21)

His most manifested expression of love came when He sacrificed Himself on the cross in front of all to save man from destruction. There was no greater expression of love than this. *(John 15:13; John 19:16-18, 30)*

Joy, rejoicing, happiness

Jesus was also very transparent about His joy, which He told His disciples so on several occasions. One came again from the Vinedresser parable in the Gospel of John, when He said, *"These things I have spoken to you so that My joy may be in you, and that your joy may be made full." (John 15:11)* Another came as they listened to a prayer He openly offered before God in their presence, *"But now I come to You; and these things I speak in the world so that they may have My joy made full in themselves." (John 17:13)*

Jesus' declaration of His own joy was not the only way He expressed it. He genuinely showed joy through His emotions when He saw others demonstrating great faith or doing good works for the kingdom. An example came early in His ministry when He marveled at the faith of a believing Roman centurion, a man who unashamedly declared his faith in Christ and His ability to heal others.

But the centurion said, "Lord, I am not worthy for You to come under my roof, but just say the word, and my servant will be healed. For I also am a man under authority, with soldiers under me; and I say to this one, 'Go!' and he goes, and to another, 'Come!' and he comes, and to my slave, 'Do this!' and he does it." Now when Jesus heard this, He marveled and said to those who were following, "Truly I say to you, I have not found such great faith with anyone in Israel." (Matthew 8:8-10)

Another way Jesus expressed His joy was through rejoicing. This was demonstrated when 70 of His disciples returned home from their first evangelistic campaign as described in the Gospel of Luke.

The seventy returned with joy, saying, "Lord, even the demons are subject to us in Your name." And He said to them, "I was watching Satan fall from heaven like lightning. Behold, I have given you authority to tread on serpents and scorpions, and over all the power of the enemy, and nothing will injure you. Nevertheless do not rejoice in this, that the spirits are subject to you, but rejoice that your names are recorded in heaven." At that very time He rejoiced greatly in the Holy Spirit, and said, "I praise You, O Father, Lord of heaven and earth, that You have hidden these things from the wise and intelligent and have revealed them to infants. Yes, Father, for this way was well-pleasing in Your sight." (Luke 10:17-21)

Anger

As open as Jesus was in sharing His love and joy before others, He was equally as open and transparent in sharing His negative feelings. He did not hide His anger as seen with the money-changers in the Temple.

The Passover of the Jews was near, and Jesus went up to Jerusalem. And He found in the temple those who were selling oxen and sheep and doves, and the moneychangers seated at their tables. And He made a scourge of cords, and drove them all out of the temple, with the sheep and the oxen; and He poured out the coins of the money changers and overturned their tables ... (John 2:13-15)

Grief and distress

Jesus didn't conceal His grief and distress either as was demonstrated in His pre-crucifixion prayers at Gethsemane.

Then Jesus came with them to a place called Gethsemane, and said to His disciples, "Sit here while I go over there and pray." And He took with Him Peter and the two sons of Zebedee, and began to be grieved and distressed. Then He said to them, "My soul is deeply grieved, to the point of death; remain here and keep watch with Me." (Matthew 26:36-38)

Sadness

Jesus didn't keep His sad times a secret, nor did He hide His tears from others. His experience with the death of Lazareth, a great friend, was proof of this.

When Jesus therefore saw her weeping, and the Jews who came with her also weeping, He was deeply moved in spirit and was troubled, and said, "Where have you laid him?" They said to Him, "Lord, come and see." Jesus wept. (John 11:33-35)

Disappointment

Jesus openly shared His disappointments, especially when His disciples didn't understand fully who He was after being with Him so long.

"If you had known Me, you would have known My Father also; from now on you know Him, and have seen Him." Philip said to Him, "Lord, show us the Father, and it is enough for us." Jesus said to him, "Have I been so long with you, and yet you have not come to know Me, Philip? He who has seen Me has seen the Father; how can you say, ' show us the Father?'" (John 14:7-9)

Disgust

Finally, in respect to the negative, Jesus was open about the things that disgusted Him. The best example was with the religious leaders of His day. Jesus didn't hesitate to criticize many of them face to face, but publicly before others, as well.

"Woe to you, scribes and Pharisees, hypocrites! For you are like whitewashed tombs, which on the outside appear beautiful, but inside they are full of dead men's bones and all uncleanness. So you, too, outwardly appear righteous to men, but inwardly you are full of hypocrisy and lawlessness. Woe to you, scribes and Pharisees, hypocrites! For you build the tombs of the prophets and adorn the monuments of the righteous..." (Matthew 23:27-29)

As you can see, Jesus was a terrific example of being open and transparent. Sometimes He built up others through it; at other times He used it to bring accountability. But regardless of how Jesus used openness and transparency, it was His desire that all of His disciples in every century follow His example. If not, He wouldn't have modeled it the way He did. You should do likewise with your children, if they are to be complete in their walk with Him, you, and others.

Parent Application

As you look at parenting applications related to openness and transparency, consider these organized under the following headings: *A Call to Openness, The Road to Transparency, Cautions,* and *Opting Out.*

A Call to Openness

As seen through the life of David and Jesus, God desires that all should be open and transparent in their Christian walk, especially Christian parents who are God's primary models of truth to their children. Many parents I have met over the years feel that it is not appropriate to share their feelings with their children. By modeling this they are indirectly telling their children to do the same. However, God doesn't want this, as explained over and over in Scripture. A truly mature Christian parent is not afraid to share the good, difficult, and even bad parts of their lives with their children. If true intimacy is going to be achieved with your children then being open and transparent is essential. If your children only see the victories or the stellar parts of your Christian life and character, then they will end up only seeing one part of who you are. Instead they need to see all of you, even the frustrations, failures, and sins that make up your life. If they don't, they won't know how to deal with similar struggles they will encounter in the years to come. They may even end up guilt-ridden, believing the Christian walk should always be victorious and triumphant, devoid of all struggle. Hardly the truth!

The Road to Transparency

There is a road to travel to accomplish transparency and openness in your parenting. It begins with encouraging your children from the start not to be afraid of sharing their sins and failures with you and others. David did this as you saw in many of his Psalms, particularly Psalm 51. When your children admit their wrongs, don't discipline them right away, but rather praise them for their openness to admit what they have done. Then share with them situations in your life where you have done something similar and how you dealt with it. Perhaps discipline is still necessary, but I would make sure it is a lot milder correction because of their openness and honesty.

Another part of the road to transparency is to encourage your children to express their joys and victories when they come in life. There is no reason to keep these quiet or under wraps; it doesn't prove anything to do so. David certainly didn't when joy and victory came to his life; he even leaped and danced on one occasion in front of others when the Ark was returned. *(II Samuel 6:16)* You may not be the leaping or dancing type, but your children may be. If so, then let them do whatever expresses their joy, even if it is different from what you would do. Remember, they are not you.

Give your children the freedom to openly share their disappointments, down times, problems, conflicts, and hard moments. These are not sins or failures; they are things that come to all because of the troubled and sinful world in which we live. Encourage them to share the things that bother them, for it is critical to their spiritual growth and essential to build an intimate relationship with you. Prohibiting them from sharing the negative because Christians aren't supposed to be negative, is just plain crazy according to the Word. Not only did David express the negative feelings of his life, so did Jesus. Even though Jesus led the most victorious life of all, He didn't hesitate to express his distressed thoughts and disappointed feelings, as shown at Gethsemane and Lazareth's funeral. *(Matthew 26:36-40)* Being positive, upbeat, and undaunted in all circumstances is not particularly a description of the victorious Christian life; rather it is being real and authentic as Jesus was. So encourage your children to share all of their feelings, both the positive and negative.

The last part of the road to transparency is to encourage your children to be open about their relationship with God. This begins by teaching them to always be honest about where they are spiritually, which will help you to support them when needed. You should lead the way in this as actions speak louder than a dozen Scripture verses thrown at them. If you don't set the example in this, but keep appearing as the one who is always *right on* spiritually, don't be surprised if they refuse to let you into that part of their life when they grow into adolescence and beyond.

Finally, you should encourage them to be transparent with others about their relationship with God. How else can the Gospel get spread to their generation unless someone is sharing it? This means that you need to do the same with your generation, that is, if you intend on being their example to follow.

Cautions

In the midst of the call to openness and transparency, there are some cautions to consider. The age, understanding, and maturity of your children determine what you can openly share or not share with them. For instance, you don't what to tell them about some of the adult issues you may have like sexual temptations or moral failures. Issues like these should be reserved for when they are young adults. You also don't want to reveal all of the daily doubts and fears you go through; keep in mind they are not your confidants and counselors, they are your children. If you are not sure what to share, then seek the advice of other Christian parents and friends, primarily those who have experience with children.

With this in view, begin telling your children bits and pieces about yourself, but once again, always keep in mind their age and maturity. Share how you came to know Christ as Savior and what your life was like before making that decision. As they get older, gradually tell them more and more about your hopes, dreams, successes, and strengths. Mix in your weaknesses, fears, disappointments, and struggles as you go.

Another caution has to do with how your children vent their negative feelings. While it is very important for them to do so, it can lead to a critical or gossipy spirit. In order to counter this, you must seek a strategy that helps your children understand God's point of view when saddened, hurt, or angered by others.

When my daughter was in junior high school, a very difficult time because of peer pressure and desire for acceptance, I helped her work out such a strategy. Shannon was in the seventh grade, and she occasionally came home at night quite discouraged because there was a clique of girls at school who wouldn't let her be a part of their group. They were the so-called popular girls at school. To make things worse, these girls accepted her best girlfriend into their group, but not Shannon. In response, my wife and I didn't just let this go, but encouraged Shannon to voice her frustrations to us as often as needed. Each time we'd sympathize and pray with her and remind Shannon again and again of her value to us, God, and many others at school. Then, I got an idea one day that settled her spirit and lessened her sadness and negative feelings. I sprung a new question on her before she could vent, one that caught her off guard. I simply asked, "So, how did it go today, how did you do with the SPGS (Pronounced spahgs)?"

Shannon quickly responded, "Dad, what are you talking about? What are SPGS?"

"You know, the girls at school who have proclaimed themselves as the popular girls on campus; <u>S</u> standing for self-proclaimed, <u>P</u> for popular, and <u>G</u> for girls.

Shannon said, "I think I get your point Dad, but tell me more, you know, so I don't miss anything."

"Well, Shannon, there's a group in every school (I knew; I was a teacher) that somehow is able to convince everyone else that they're the *cool ones* on campus. And then for some dumb reason, everyone believes that and accepts them as such. But this acceptance only lasts for a few years, because most of the other kids end up not caring anymore, for they have found friends they love and love being with. Pathetically the SPGS keep trying to be popular, but it's a losing effort for them because by the time high school is over, no one really cares. So, Shannon how are the SPGS doing today?"

"Pretty SPGY Dad, pretty SPGY." We both laughed, and soon after the SPGS hurts and angers faded away.

So, why was this lesson so effective in changing Shannon's thinking and heart? First of all we let her vent her negative feelings about the SPGS for quite awhile, but we didn't let her work herself into a critical spirit. Our prayers with her brought God constantly into the picture, which gave her the strength she needed. Because of His strength, she continued in the midst of her disgust to show love toward these girls, even though it was hardly ever returned. The prayers also set the stage in her heart to hear the timely lesson I shared about the SPGS.

What happened as the years passed? The SPGS did pretty much as I predicted, and the compassion for others Shannon learned during this whole experience was probably the key to her later becoming the Junior Class President and then the Student Body President of her high school. I think those who voted for her sensed her empathy and oneness with them, which was quite devoid of SPGNESS.

Opting Out

Even though there are clear examples in Scripture, many Christian parents choose to opt out of being open and transparent with their children. They do so for a couple of unfortunate reasons. Some fear they would lose a grip on their authority as a parent if they did. They feel admitting wrongs and weaknesses would cause disrespect. This is problematic for the very opposite is true. As time passes, many of these parents end up having incredible problems with their kids, who like them, hide what is truly going on in their lives.

Other parents who opt out of openness and transparency simply don't want to be viewed as anything but perfect in their children's eyes. To their discredit, they are more concerned with how they appear to their children, than what is good for their kids. They too may have tremendous problems with their children later on.

So don't opt out of openness and transparency; instead, let your children occasionally hear words from you like, "I'm sorry," "I have done wrong," or "please forgive me." They need to hear these words, because these expressions speak of your humility. And as the Scripture teaches, humility begets humility, which will cause your children to listen to you all the more as you teach them God's Word. *(James 5:16)*

Final Thoughts

In the opening story about Gary and my youth group, the practice of openness and transparency was never more evident than at our Sunday night *Body Life* meetings. It was truly a snapshot of what I wanted to do with my children in the years to come, and what I believe all parents should experience with theirs.

After almost every song on those evenings at my house, many of the kids opened up and shared both the good and bad of their lives with each other. In return they received compassion, understanding, support, and prayers. Because of this we drew closer and closer to one another, as will happen with you and your children should you apply such openness and transparency in your parenting. If many in our youth group are still close to one another today after only spending three or four years together, can you imagine what your relationship with your children will be after you spend most of your life with them?

Teachable Moment

When children are born into this world, they come naturally to us with open and transparent hearts. Some say they are this way because they don't know any better. But this is the way God created children from the beginning. I believe they would remain so if we didn't educate it out of them.

This open and honest nature causes them to hug at a moments notice, cry when hurt, believe without doubt, cheer when you show up, say they are sorry when they have done wrong, cry for you when you are sad, ask for help when stuck, and express a full measure of love no matter who your are or what you've done.

So, for this Teachable Moment look to your children as examples to follow when they are being transparent. Let their honest and unreserved expressions remind you of what you need to be with others in this respect, particularly those in your family. Of course you don't want to emulate the negative parts of their transparency like screaming when things don't go well, but much of the rest you do.

The following verses referenced in this chapter can be found in sequence on my web site, www.tmoments.com. Click on the Book Resources button located on the home page.

Psalm 38:1-8; Psalm 139:5; John 15:13; John 19:16-18, 30; John 15:11; John 17:13; II Samuel 6:16; Matthew 26:36-40; James 5:16

SEVEN
FILING AWAY
ENCOURAGEMENTS
(Encouraging your children)

He makes me lie down in green pastures; He leads me beside quiet waters. He restores my soul.
(Psalm 23:2, 3)

The third component to build intimacy with your children is the practice of encouragement. Parents who know how to encourage effectively usually end up with kids who develop confidence in themselves, in their parents, and in God. However, encouraging children is not something that comes naturally to all parents. For many, it must be learned. The reason is that encouragement is often a varying blend of circumstances, affirming actions, and uplifting words.

To help you better understand, I will analyze the encouragement David gave his sheep while resting in green pastures near cool waters, along with how God personally encouraged him. Jesus' ministry of encouragement, on the other hand, will be viewed in context with His work with Peter right before his three denials.

David

David knew as a young shepherd a sheep's need for rest and encouragement; understanding that the trails they often traveled together were filled with a variety of difficult circumstances, setbacks, and disappointments. There were predators to worry about, food and water to secure, injuries to mend, weather to contend with, and mistakes to account for and correct. On a daily basis, one, a few, or several of these caused David's sheep to experience discouragement. In response, David did many things to encourage and affirm his flock, often resting them in a green pasture, near a cool stream.[1] During these times, he moved amongst each of his sheep calming their spirits with his harp and songs, inspiring them with uplifting words, and rubbing their heads to show affection.[2,3] He applied some of these same shepherding skills with King Saul while serving him.

FILING AWAY ENCOURAGEMENT

"Let our lord now command your servants who are before you. Let them seek a man who is a skillful player on the harp; and it shall come about when the evil spirit from God is on you, that he shall play the harp with his hand, and you will be well." Then one of the young men said, "Behold, I have seen a son of Jesse who is a skillful musician, a mighty man of valor, a warrior, one prudent in speech, and a handsome man; and the Lord is with him." So Saul sent messengers to Jesse and said, "Send me your son David who is with the flock." (I Samuel 16:16, 18-19)

As encouraging as David was with his sheep and King Saul, God did so much more with him during the course of his life. Here are just a couple of David's words of appreciation after being uplifted and affirmed by God and His Word.

I will extol You, my God, O King, and I will bless Your name forever and ever. Every day I will bless You, and I will praise Your name forever and ever. Great is the LORD, and highly to be praised… (Psalm 145:1-3)

How precious also are Your thoughts to me, O God! How vast is the sum of them. (Psalm 139:17)

These words and others like them throughout the Scripture can serve as examples of what to share with your children as they go through the difficulties of their lives.

Jesus

The encouraging comments God gave His beloved children throughout the Scripture were numerous, constant, and always timely. One of the most affirming and uplifting comments was given to Peter right before Jesus' trials and crucifixion. The circumstance leading to Jesus' conversation with Peter began with a confrontation with the religious leaders. In Jesus' debate with them, they demanded that He produce a miraculous sign from heaven to prove who He was. *(Matthew 16:1-4)* Jesus refused, but He later took their question and asked Peter and the other disciples who they thought He was? After a few tried to answer, Peter stepped forth and said, *"You are the Christ, the Son of the living God."* Jesus was impressed, even though He knew the Father had implanted those thoughts within Peter. *(Matthew 16:13-17)* This didn't prevent Jesus from saying some very encouraging and affirming things to him. He called Peter a rock; a picturesque way of saying his faith was strong. Jesus went on and told him that the coming church would be founded on what he had just declared, and that hell itself wouldn't prevail against it. Jesus finished by telling Peter that what he was going to do on earth would also count in heaven.

> *"I also say to you that you are Peter, and upon this rock I will build My church; and the gates of Hades will not overpower it. I will give you the keys of the kingdom of heaven; and whatever you bind on earth shall have been bound in heaven, and whatever you loose on earth shall have been loosed in heaven." (Matthew 16:18-19)*

Comments like these obviously helped and inspired Peter very much, but why did Jesus tell him these affirming things when He did? Because not many days later as Jesus predicted, Peter was going to deny Him before others and then hide until His crucifixion was over. *(Matthew 26:31-34)* Knowing this and sensing the great failure and depression Peter was about to experience, Jesus saw fit to let him know before hand the good He saw in him. What Jesus said worked, for Peter sought the Lord after the resurrection and served Him mightily the rest of his life. *(John 21:7)*

If you follow Christ's example with your children, encouraging them with uplifting words, you will not only bring them joy and confidence as Jesus did with Peter, but you will also remind them of their value to you and God.

Parent Application

The parent applications for encouragement are organized under the following headings: *Carrying Out Consistent Encouragement, Heartening Comments Help in Tough Times, Encouraging through Mistakes, Exaggerating Your Comments,* and *Encouraging Other Children.*

Carrying out Consistent Encouragement

Consistent encouragement is important when developing intimacy with your children. In addition to saying positive things throughout a day, a special time should be periodically planned to give them an extended dose of encouragement. This is likened to what David did when taking his sheep from one green pasture to the other to be restored and encouraged.

Without a good dose of regular encouragement, the possibility of your children falling prey to constant discouragements of this world is great, for they live in a world filled with criticism, ego, anger, and hurt.

During these regular times, come up with affirming comments that will remind your children of the good things you see in them. Then mention at least one affirmation from Scripture that shows God's view and perspective about them. Here are some from which to draw:

You are the salt of the earth. (Matthew 5:13)

You are the light of the world. (Matthew 5:14)

You are My child. (John 1:12)

You are a part of Me, a channel of My life. (John 15:5)

You are My friend. (John 15:15)

You are chosen to bear fruit for Me. (John 15:16)

You are a joint heir with Me; everything that is mine is Yours. (Romans 8:16-17)

You are a temple, a dwelling place where I hang out. (I Corinthians 3:16, 6:19; rbk)

You are united with Me. (I Corinthians 6:15)

You are a member of My church. (I Corinthians 12:27; Ephesians 5:30)

You are a new creation. (II Corinthians 5:17)

You are chosen of God, holy and dearly loved. (Colossians 3:12; I Thessalonians 1:4)

You are a son of light and not darkness. (I Thessalonians 5:5)

You are like a Godly living stone, being built up in Me as a spiritual house. (I Peter 2:5)

You are one of My wonderful works. (Psalm 139:13-14)

You are a member of the chosen race, a royal priesthood, a holy nation, a people for God's own possession. (I Peter 2:9)

Heartening Comments Help in Tough Times

Heartening and encouraging comments embedded within the hearts of your children can help them get through tough times, particularly times when others criticize and tear them down. During such instances, their only resource to survive could be what you have told them about themselves, as well as what God has said through His Word. Accordingly, just as Jesus told Peter he was a rock before the crowds came after him, do the same for your children.

Encouraging through Mistakes

At different times, your children will make a variety of mistakes. Some will require your discipline, others your encouragement. You will have to get into the hearts of your children and find out why they did what they did to determine whether discipline or encouragement is needed. If their mistake was not a result of disobedience, sin, or rebellion, then encourage them. I saw an example of this a number of years ago when watching my son's high school volleyball team play. Unlike any sport I'd ever seen, volleyball players on both sides encouraged their teammates no matter what mistake was made. And even if a player badly blew a play, his teammates often encouraged him all the more so he wouldn't stay discouraged. On account of this, most players recovered quickly and did much better as the match progressed. I suggest you do likewise with your children, encourage them through mistakes, don't dwell or harp on their miscues or failures.

Exaggerating Your Comments

Words of encouragement need to be genuine, just as they were with Gary, the young boy who had cancer in the opening story. Each in our youth group expressed to God their individual reasons for sparing Gary's life. No one in the group hyped what they said for the sake of making Gary feel better. Every word was straightforward, honest, and truthful. Your words should be just as genuine when encouraging your children.

Surprisingly, when it comes to bestowing genuine encouragement, some parents give way to exaggeration when complimenting their children's feats and performances. One of the realities of this life is that very few children are proficient, talented, or gifted in everything they do. Unless yours is the exception, then strive to be genuine when complimenting them. Pile the praise on only if your children really do well in something. This does not mean you shouldn't applaud them while trying different things; just don't exaggerate your comments. Until you know in what they will truly excel, stick with phrases like: *"Hang in there," "Do your best," "Good effort,"* or *"Nice try."* Stay away from embellished phrases like: *"You are the best," "No one does this as well as you," "You're perfect,"* or *"You've outdone everyone."* The goal is to genuinely uplift your children, not artificially inflate their egos toward conceit and ungodly pride.

Encouraging Other Children

In addition to encouraging your children with timely words and praises, don't forget there may be other children God may bring across your path that need to be uplifted, too. They may be nephews and nieces, friends of your children, neighborhood kids, or children at church. Due to family situations, they may not have anyone who builds them up, or sees the good in them. Therefore, don't hesitate to play the role of encourager with these kids, too. You might be the only one who does.

As I mentioned earlier, I grew up in a broken home where not everything I did was appreciated as I had hoped; so from time to time, God sent someone along to say just the right comment at the right time. One of the many examples of this came during my senior year in high school. The encouragement involved basketball, a sport I loved playing and at which I worked very hard. Unfortunately for me, my high school team (Pasadena High School) was filled with talented players, who in my eyes were a lot better than me. The team was so talented that during my final year at school, our basketball team barely lost the championship in California, and only because our star center was sick for the game. Amazingly, out of the 17 players on the team, I think 12 received basketball scholarships of one kind or another; that's how good we were.

When the season was over, most of the players in the school gathered together to play every afternoon in an organized spring league. Mr. Terzian, the coach, sponsored this league and even officiated many of the games. It was quite competitive as some players like myself still felt they had something to prove. As the weeks rolled by, it finally came to an end. I was walking out of the gym on the last day when Mr. Terzian grabbed my arm and said, "Wait a minute, Kent, I want to talk to you. You played pretty well out there this spring, and I believe I missed seeing just how good you really were as a player. Sorry for that, my mistake, don't give up, good luck next year." I looked down for a moment and then said, "Thanks, coach, that means a lot, especially coming from you." As I walked away, my heart melted, for what he told me that afternoon encouraged me so much that I could hardly hold it inside. All I can say is that from then on I played with a new confidence, just because of what one person said at the right moment to encourage.

Final Thoughts

If you affirm and build up your children as you should, don't be surprised if they do the same for you one day. The Scripture teaches that what you give, you will receive, and that includes the bestowing of encouragement.

Now this I say... he who sows bountifully will also reap bountifully.
(II Corinthians 9:6)

Teachable Moment

To help remember the contents of this chapter, instead of picking something visual to help you, I suggest something a little different this time around. This illustration actually came from a joke I heard a preacher make a number of years ago. In the middle of his sermon on encouragement, he shared that when discouraged, he would pull out a folder with all of the positive letters he had received over the years. With a very serious expression, he then said that both of these letters encouraged him as his mother and wife said some very good things about him. Of course, all of us listening laughed because he was a very popular and well-liked preacher. If he had such a folder, it would have been filled with thousands of encouraging letters.

When I got home and was having my devotions the next morning, I thought about his folder illustration, even though it was meant as a joke. The more I thought about it, the more it sounded like a good idea to fend off discouragement. So, I put one together for myself and have added to it now for 15 years. It has helped over the years. When I get down, I read one of those old letters or comments people made, and it would often uplift my spirit.

For this Teachable Moment, I suggest you do the same with each member in your family, especially your children. Their folders should include anything said to or about them that will build them up. This might start with the positive notes received from school, friends, Sunday school teachers, coaches, and other extended family members. It could include good things said of them in their birthday cards. Can you imagine how big this file could become if they began amassing it right now while they are young. More importantly, can you imagine how they will feel after re-reading some of these encouraging comments, especially when they are struggling or down on themselves? Encouraged, I would think; try it!

The following verses referenced in this chapter can be found in sequence on my web site, www.tmoments.com. Click on the Book Resources button located on the home page.

Matthew 16:1-4; Matthew 16:13-17; Matthew 26:31-34; John 21:7

EIGHT
AGAPE LOVE

(Achieving intimacy through the two sides of love)

…Your rod and staff, they comfort me. (rbk)
(Psalm 23:4)

Agape love is the fourth component to building intimacy with your children, and perhaps the hardest to achieve because it deals with applying just the right amount of discipline and grace. *Agape* is the Greek word for love used throughout the original texts of the Scripture to describe God's unconditional love for us.[1]

A coin is a good illustration of what *Agape* love is because it has two sides to it, a head and a tail. The head side being the application of discipline and the tail being grace. In Scripture as well as in parenting, sometimes discipline (head) is used more than grace (tail), and sometimes the opposite. Regardless of which is used more, discipline and grace are equal in importance, and both are needed when working with your children's behavior.

Before discussing *Agape* love, I have a personal story to share where the two sides of it were demonstrated in a rather dramatic way when teaching school a number of years ago. The story mostly deals with a boy named Tom, but it is also about an all-knowing God, a faithful father, and a very good class.

Tom

Tom was just 11 years old when he entered my sixth grade class in the middle of the 1988 school year. He came from a divorced home where there had been a lot of turmoil and hurt. Both of Tom's parents came from Christian homes, but for a variety of reasons, this influence didn't help them when important choices had to be made concerning their marriage and raising Tom.

After a difficult divorce, Tom's mother was granted full custody but struggled raising a boy on her own. She had to work to make ends meet, so she had little time for Tom. As Tom developed through those early years, he became more and more out of control. Several times he was suspended from different schools for a variety of behavioral reasons. After much consternation and frustration, his mother finally decided to send him to his father. Tom's father was a very kind man and thrilled to take him, but like his ex-wife, lacked experience raising a boy, particularly one lacking self-control.

After a year of trying to be a good father, he found that all his efforts with Tom were also failing. When he was at his lowest, he prayed and prayed asking God for help. Soon after, an idea came to him that perhaps Tom could be rescued by the same Christian school that turned his own life around when he was a young boy.

So he called the Christian school at which I was teaching. To his surprise, the sixth grade teacher who rescued him was now the school principal. After pleading his case, the principal considered enrolling Tom. He then approached me with the situation and asked if I would take Tom even though it was in the middle of the year. I thought about it for awhile and came back and said, "Sure, I'll take him." How could I do otherwise? After all my own sixth grade teacher, Mrs. Dean, did the same for me when I was struggling like Tom.

Before Tom was allowed to come to class, I asked for a meeting with his dad. I explained that there wouldn't be any guarantees and that Tom would be treated like the other children, with discipline and grace. Tom's dad readily agreed and voiced his willingness to do anything on his end to make this work. He was true to his word as we began meeting together on a regular basis to see what we could do to get Tom's heart changed, both at school and at home.

Things didn't start off well for Tom; he was out of control from the *get go*. He had a lot going against himself because sixth grade normally was a tough year for most students anyway. It's the beginning of adolescence, an in-between stage in life, where kids begin to transition into adulthood physically and emotionally but are still children in many ways.[2] On top of that Tom was coming into class during the middle of the year without a friend in the world and a lot to catch up on academically. However, my class was very special that year. In fact, I had never had a class like them before in my teaching career. They were so kind and accommodating, always reaching out to help one another.

When Tom arrived, I know he was surprised when they immediately treated him like a long lost friend. I know this because I could see it on his face those first few days. Sad to say, though, his true character and work habits soon came out when he started lying, cheating, failing in his school work, and getting into fights with boys from other classes.

Even so, I didn't give up on him, applying discipline and grace when needed. Yet month after month, he still didn't change much, especially in regard to lying. Now, lying was a big issue to me, not just with Tom but with everyone in class. In fact, no matter what students did, if they told the truth, they would receive a different set of consequences from me.

I called it my *Plan A and B* consequences, which were based on two parts of Agape love, the mercy part of grace (not getting what you deserve) and discipline (getting the full measure of what you deserve). I explained it this way to my students, including Tom, "If you do something wrong and tell the truth, then you'll receive *Plan A,"* typically a lesser consequence. "If you lie, then you receive *Plan B* a much heavier consequence, not only for the wrong done but lying about it too." I then said I wouldn't tell them ahead of time the consequences for *Plan A or B*, so they would just have to make their best choice, hopefully the honest one.

As you might have guessed, Tom lived pretty much according to *Plan B* throughout the school year. He simply couldn't tell the truth about anything or admit that he had done wrong. I cannot tell you how many recesses he missed, how many days he had to stay after school, or how many times his father grounded him because he wouldn't tell the truth.

During the last two months of school, Tom's dad and I decided to intensify our efforts to get to his heart, which was all we were ever after. We worked out a system where I filled out a report on Tom at the end of every week, If he behaved, his dad rewarded him by taking him to McDonalds on the weekend, a place Tom loved to go. The first week worked, Tom got to go, but he then slipped back into his old ways missing one date at McDonald's after the next. Frustrating to say the least! As the year came to a close, it looked like nothing had worked to get through to Tom's heart. I was very disappointed, and so was his dad.

Then with only about four weeks to go, something dramatic happened, something I believe the Lord orchestrated. One day while I stepped out of class, Tom really exploded in frustration to his classmates exclaiming with a loud voice, "Dr. McClain doesn't like me, he is always punishing me." Several students quickly responded with something like this, "No, that's not true Tom. We know Dr. McClain and if he's really not happy with you, he won't say much. Tom! Dr. McClain must really like you because he's talking to you all the time." For some reason, that ended up being the pivotal point for Tom. His behavior began to improve in class and on the playground. As wonderful as that was to see, the best was still to come during the last week of school.

Two days before school was to end, Tom reverted back to his old ways and got into a scuffle with another boy on the playground during recess, and I had actually witnessed it from the second row balcony at our school. As the students rolled into class after the break, they began telling me of the incident, but I stopped them in midstream and said, "I know, I saw it all." I was sad because Tom had been doing so well, and I knew when I confronted him, he would lie about it. I was already thinking up what the *Plan B* consequence would be, even though I didn't want to discipline him just before school ended. As Tom came into the room, I said, "Tom, stay outside for a minute. We need to talk." I put the class to work, but all were watching out the window with great curiosity. I said, "Now, Tom, I have knowledge that you got into a fight of sorts on the playground, is this true?

Tom put his head down for a while, then looked up and said, "Yes, Dr. McClain, I pushed a boy at recess which got us into a fight. I am the one who started it all. I shouldn't have, but I did, and I'm sorry."

I was a bit taken back and then exclaimed, "Tom, you told me the truth!" I think my students inside the classroom heard me, I was a bit excited. "Since you did, Tom, *Plan A* and not *Plan B* will be your consequence."

With his head still hanging low, he said, "What's that, Dr. McClain?"

"Well, Tom, you need to apologize to the boy you pushed and don't do it again."

"And that's it, Dr. McClain, that's *Plan A*?"

"Yea, that's it, Tom."

"Wow," he uttered in a very low and peaceful voice. Tom made things right with the boy as soon as he could and spent the last day at school with a joy in him I had never before seen.

Tom stayed at our school another two years before he moved. During that time, I know his dad continued to do a credible job in applying both discipline and grace with him. Every once and awhile, Tom would come by my classroom to report on how he was doing in junior high. We ended up with a great relationship and had many good talks. At the end of his eighth grade year, he was chosen by his teachers and administrators to be the school's student of the month because of his outstanding Christian example at school. Quite a change, don't you think?

What's Ahead?

Agape love and its two sides of discipline and grace are so important in raising your children that the next two chapters have been dedicated to it. The core references of David and Jesus remain, with particular emphasis on the rod and staff in David's Psalm 23. *(Psalm 23:4)*

Final Thoughts

When changing the heart of a child, sometimes it takes more of one side of Agape love than another to do it; at least for a season. With Tom, the discipline side had to be used a great deal at first, but when his heart began to change, grace was quickly ushered in to keep him on the right path. As to Tom's years in high school and beyond I don't know, but I'll bet he lived more on the grace side of Agape.

The following verses referenced in this chapter can be found in sequence on my web site, www.tmoments.com. Click on the Book Resources button located on the home page.

Psalm 23:4

NINE

THE ROD OF DISCIPLINE

(Applying the appropriate amount of discipline and correction)

Even though I walk through the valley of the shadow of death, I fear no evil, for You are with me; Your rod...comforts me. (rbk)
(Psalm 23:4)

Disciplining and correcting children for most parents is neither comfortable nor easy to carry out, because it requires taking negative actions like reprimands, restrictions, and other types of punishment. Consequently, this side of the Agape love coin must be accomplished with great understanding and balance; otherwise, it might be underdone or overdone. If underdone, your disciplinary efforts can lead to terrible behavior and havoc in the home. If your discipline is overdone, it can cause your children to develop a fear of you, hardly a basis for an intimate and lasting relationship with them.

To arrive at a healthy way to discipline, one that will help your children mature and thrive, we will look at what David meant when he wrote in Psalm 23, "*Your rod comforts me.*" Then we will move on to Jesus and see how effectively and lovingly He disciplined and corrected His disciples.

David

David illustrated the discipline and protection God gave him throughout his life with the rod he used in his shepherding duties.[1] When he used the rod well with his sheep, they were strengthened and comforted, as well as being shielded from all kinds of harm. The same was felt by David when God used His loving rod with him. *(II Samuel 22:2-3)*

David's rod looked something like a policeman's club or modern day baseball bat and was usually held in one hand with a taller staff in the other. It was a formidable weapon; predators usually kept their distance upon seeing it.[2] As important as the rod was for protection, it had an even greater value as an instrument for correction with David's flocks. For instance, some of the mountain trails on which David led his sheep were quite narrow and dangerous.[3] If David's sheep didn't carefully walk on the inside of the trails as instructed, then a drift or defiant move to the outside could end their lives through a fall down the mountainside. David had several choices to make to keep this from happening, which included various levels of discipline like scolding, using the rod, and even breaking a sheep's hind legs if necessary.[4] Breaking a sheep's leg sounds cruel, but if a particular sheep was so rebellious, influencing other sheep to be the same, then this had to be done so the whole flock wouldn't perish over the side of a mountain. Such discipline was painful as you might imagine, but it was more painful for the shepherd who was duty-bound to carry the rebellious sheep on his shoulders until the legs healed.[5] He did so because he was committed to all of his sheep, even to the most rebellious.

It is assumed that David, like all good shepherds of his day, carried out these disciplines in a progressive manner, gradually moving from the least corrective discipline to the next according to the sheep's infraction, circumstance, or past history. Presumably, this was carried out with a rationale not to scare the sheep into obedience but rather love them into it. Therefore, it was highly unlikely David struck his sheep with the rod for every infraction but progressively did only what was necessary to change their hearts. When this was accomplished, the discipline ceased for the goal had been achieved.

In David's life, God also progressively disciplined him. Although David did many good things for God, he also did many things that were very sinful, as admitted in Psalm 32. However, God didn't bring the rod down on him every time he blew it. Instead He used a variety of corrective measures to change David's heart, sometimes just forgiving him upon confession. You need to consider doing likewise with your own children, for the rod of discipline never means carrying out the harshest of punishments every time.

How blessed is he whose transgression is forgiven, whose sin is covered! How blessed is the man to whom the Lord does not impute iniquity, and in whose spirit there is no deceit! When I kept silent about my sin, my body wasted away through my groaning all day long. For day and night Your hand was heavy upon me; my vitality was drained away as with the fever heat of summer. I acknowledged my sin to You, and my iniquity I did not hide; I said, "I will confess my transgressions to the Lord; and You forgave the guilt of my sin." (Psalm 32:1-5)

In some circumstances (and this is conjecture), it is possible David did nothing as one of his disciplinary or corrective measures. Such inaction wasn't because he had grown soft or permissive but to let his sheep reap the consequences of their own actions. If a particular sheep had the propensity to walk too closely to the outer edge of a trail, he might have allowed it to fall off the trail if it wasn't too dangerous to do so. By such inaction, the sheep learned more by the fall then by David's warning or tap on the tail with his rod. This certainly happened with David when God didn't punish him right away for his adulterous affair with Bathsheba. He simply let him go on sinning for awhile, bearing the consequences of his own actions. When David was through sinning, he then had to deal with heartache and the shame of adultery, murder, and losing a child. Yet, he repented after seeing what he had done and God forgave him. *(II Samuel 11:1-5, 13-14)* He was never the same afterward, which was good, for he needed a change of heart to finish the work God had called him to do on earth.

Finally, in regard to David's discipline with his flock, progressive steps would have been thrown out if a particular sheep was in peril. To save it, he wouldn't have hesitated to immediately use the harshest measure of his rod or even his sling shot to save its life.[6, 7, 8] Likewise, in some cases with your children, you may have to use the harshest measure of discipline to keep them from personal disaster. Just don't use it all the time; God didn't with David and neither should you with your children.

Jesus

Jesus, who was often referred to as the good shepherd, employed similar measures of discipline and correction with His disciples. How He went about this was analogous to David's use of the rod with his sheep. As David used the rod to tap or rap a sheep's backside to get it moving or corrected, so did Jesus with the disciples to move them forward spiritually.

A tap from Jesus' rod included an array of different rebukes. An example of one came in the midst of a storm on the Sea of Galilee, a situation where the disciples had an opportunity to trust Him, but didn't. (Mark 4:37-40) Even though Jesus was in the boat with them during a storm, they panicked and lost their faith and confidence in Him. In response, Jesus didn't rap them hard with a harsh criticism, nor suspend or separate them from being His disciples, but He did express deep disappointment. This was all that was needed to get them back on track, which at times may be all you will need to do with your children.

At other times, Jesus rapped the disciples a little harder with discipline, not just with harsher words but by letting them bear the consequences of their own actions. An example of this came when Peter tried to walk on the Sea of Galilee as Jesus had done, but did so according to his own strength. For a few moments Jesus did nothing, letting Peter sink before rescuing him. He then followed up with an appropriate rebuke. *(Matthew 14:28-31)*

In addition to the different steps Jesus used with His discipline, there were harsher ones He and the rest of the Trinity (Father and Spirit) applied as indicated in the books of Hebrews and Lamentations. Sometimes, the discipline was like a scourging, at other times it was laden with grief-producing consequences.

For those whom the Lord loves He disciplines, and He scourges every son whom He receives. It is for discipline that you endure; God deals with you as with sons; for what son is there whom his father does not discipline? (Hebrews 12:7-8)

All discipline for the moment seems not to be joyful, but sorrowful; yet to those who have been trained by it, afterwards it yields the peaceful fruit of righteousness. (Hebrews 12:11)

For if He causes grief, then He will have compassion according to His abundant lovingkindness. For He does not afflict willingly or grieve the sons of men. (Lamentations 3:32-33)

Parent Application

When considering the rod of discipline for correction, here are some parenting applications drawn from Scriptures about David, Jesus, and others; they are organized under the following headings: *Directing a Child's Heart, Loving while Disciplining, Discarding Fear Tactics, Taking Your Time, Matching Misdeeds with the Right Consequences,* and *Following a Progressive Plan of Correction.*

Directing a Child's Heart

The primary goal of discipline is not to punish your children for every wrong or foolish deed but to create within them a heart that wants to do right. Therefore, if such a heart change happens, even in the middle of the discipline, you certainly have the option to end the discipline, for your goal has been accomplished. David likely did this as most shepherds of his day would have done, with repentant sheep. God also did the same throughout the Bible exemplified by what He did with those in Nineveh in Jonah's day. As the Scripture reports, the people of Nineveh repented after being warned, and this moved God to immediately relent of the discipline planned for them. *(Jonah 3:4-10)*

In my parenting there were several times I chose not to complete a promised consequence. I decided on this change of course because I became convinced that my kids had a change of heart and had learned their lessons.

Are there drawbacks to cutting discipline short? Yes, especially if your children have learned the art of faking heart change to get out of consequences. If they do this you will soon see it by their actions. If this ends up being the case (and I hope not), don't shorten their consequences the next time around. On a final note, I never shortened consequences when my kids physically hurt one another or others. I applied in principle the full measure of the Mosaic Law without grace. *(Deuteronomy 19:11-13)*

Loving while Disciplining

When your children misbehave, you need to discipline them accordingly. While carrying this out you should never love them less during this time of discipline than when they are obedient. Ideally, whether their behavior is bad or good, the love you have for your children needs to be constant. You must fight the temptation to love them less when they are disobedient. If you don't your love may become conditional, saying in essence, "I'll love you more if you meet my behavioral expectations, but less so if you don't." God certainly didn't love this way with David, nor did Jesus with His disciples. In both biblical accounts, unconditional love was the only love expressed, which says, "I love you no matter what you do."

In my experience as a youth pastor, I saw many young people grow up in homes where parents loved their children on a conditional basis. If their kids were obedient, they were loved and accepted; if not, they weren't. Some of these kids struggled tremendously because of this, giving up on being loved the way they were meant to. Others survived only because they latched onto those who loved them unconditionally or because of what they absorbed from the Scriptures, which expresses God's love.

Love is patient and kind. It is not provoked and doesn't take into account when wrong suffered. Love bears all things, believes all things, hopes all things, and endures all things. It never fails. (I Corinthians 13:4-5, 7-8)

To set your mind at rest, loving your kids when they are disobedient doesn't mean you can't get frustrated, disgusted, or even angry in a righteous sense with them, just never to the point where you withdraw your love. One way to keep from doing this is to state your love to them during every discipline. Tell them you don't like what they have done and because of it they will have to be disciplined, but you still love them. You may not always feel like saying those words, but say them anyway, asking God under your breath to help you mean it. Then, let God do His work both in your children and you.

Another suggestion to keep from withdrawing your love is to forget as soon as you can what they have done, moving on to something else as if what they did hadn't happened. Ask God once again to help you; ask Him to give you the same forgetful mind He has toward your past sins.

For I will be merciful to their iniquities, and I will remember their sins no more. (Hebrews 8:12)

Discarding Fear Tactics

The discipline you employ with your children should seldom, if ever, use fear tactics to change their behavior or hearts. If you do, then as the Scripture says, it can hurt the intimate love you are trying to build with them.

There is no fear in love; but perfect love casts out fear, because fear involves punishment, and the one who fears is not perfected in love. (I John 4:18)

When David said in his Psalm 23 the rod comforts, he was saying in part that the way God disciplined him eventually brought calm to his life, not anxiety or fear. Your discipline, no matter how punitive it might have to be from time to time, should bring a similar calm. If your discipline brings a calm spirit, then you are perfecting your children in love, but if not, don't be surprised if they rebel against you when they are older. Then how will you make them behave?

Taking Your Time

Discipline is not always a speedy process; sometimes it takes a long time to change a child's disobedient heart. David had to be patient with his sheep, just as God was with him, and as you will have to be with your children. An example of such patience for me was a long process of correction I had to go through with my son when he was young. When Brodie was in second grade, he was very disruptive in the classroom. While sitting down to talk with my son's teacher one day, I could tell he was frustrated with Brodie. So I asked Mr. Beachum if I could drop by several afternoons to see what my son was doing, and he readily agreed, saying, "Come as often as you can." When I did, I usually slid into the classroom and hid in the back so my son wouldn't be aware of my presence. Sure enough, Brodie was every bit as disruptive as described. After he got home from school, his mother and I had a long talk with him in our family room. I took the lead and explained to Brodie what I had seen in the classroom and how disappointed I was. I then told him it was going to stop.

I set forth a correction plan to back up my words, one that included the rod of discipline and the staff of grace, mercy, and forgiveness, which will be expanded upon in the next chapter. The plan was simple and purposed to change his heart, not just his behavior in the classroom. I told Brodie that I would come to his classroom at the end of each day to get a report from Mr. Beachum. Before explaining the consequences he would receive should the report be bad, I told him what he could expect if it was a good one. A good day would bring great praise, but three good days during a week earned him a trip to McDonalds on the weekend (the same incentive I suggested to Tom's dad in the opening story). I told Brodie if he got four good reports in a week, I would not only take him to McDonalds, but I would also put those four days on a chart. If he had many good days piled up over the next few months, I would take him on a ministry trip to Seattle with me that was coming up. He really wanted to go because he loved flying and knew I made trips fun no matter what the purpose.

On the other hand, if he had bad reports from his teacher, the following consequences would result. First, he was allowed one bad day a week without any consequences. For the second and third days of poor behavior, he would be grounded from play. If he got four or more bad reports in a week, then a spanking awaited him on Fridays. I usually didn't discipline him during the weekends; he had too many sports and other activities, and besides, he needed a break from the discipline. If I had to spank him, which I conservatively and carefully did, I made sure our relationship was restored afterward. Sometimes I did so with a hug and a "I love you, son." At other times, I waited for awhile to let the discipline sink in a little longer, but never beyond an hour or so.

I'm glad to report that Brodie's behavior in the classroom changed after a few months, and he was able to go on that trip with me to Seattle. We had a great time! After his second grade year, his behavior improved at school. It was not perfect, by any means, but enough so to dispense with this plan and all the reports. As I look back, opting to take time with Brodie's discipline was one of the best decisions I made as a parent. I encourage you to do the same when your children have behavioral challenges. The more time given to correct them the better.

Matching Misdeeds with the Right Consequences

When disciplining your children, to the best of your ability match what they have done wrong with a fair and equal consequence. If you think that only one or two consequences work in all situations, then you are mistaken. The Bible doesn't support this; just look at all the different consequences outlined in the Old Testament in respect to breaking its various laws. Capital punishment, for instance, was given only to those who committed the most serious acts of disobedience like murder. Other lesser acts of wrong doing were given lesser punishments that matched the offence.

> *If a man injures his neighbor, just as he has done, so it shall be done to him, fracture for fracture, eye for eye, and tooth for tooth; just as he has injured a man, so it shall be inflicted on him. Thus the one who kills an animal shall make it good, but the one who kills a man shall be put to death. (Leviticus 24:19-21)*

Can you imagine God primarily using capital punishment for every offence committed against Him and others? Some parents do this in a parallel sense by giving their children the harshest of consequences no matter the offence. On the other hand, can you imagine God only giving a light rebuke or slap on the wrist for every sin, no matter how gross? Yet, some parents do this too with their children.

In both cases, discipline can be overdone or underdone, so to get it right, pray, continue to read the Word, and seek out wisdom from other Christian parents. Then, apply what you have learned. Who knows, perhaps one day others will seek your advice because of the great job you have done with your children.

Following a Progressive Plan of Correction

To apply the rod of discipline to your children's misbehavior, it should be progressive, graduating from one corrective measure to the next until the heart is changed. Of course this progression needs to coordinate with the staff of grace, mercy, and forgiveness, which will be discussed in the next chapter.

The rod's progression starts with a lighter set of consequences before moving to heavier ones. This is similar in principle to the way Jesus worked with others, David did with his sheep, and God did with David. The lighter consequences might include constructive criticisms, reproofs and reprimands. If these don't work, you might move to more medium range consequences, such as revoking privileges, time outs (isolation), sterner rebukes, or letting them bear the consequences of their own actions. Sometimes it's best to allow your children to learn right from wrong through the circumstances they have created for themselves, letting them reap what they sowed. *(Galatians 6:7)* It worked for Jesus with the disciples, and it can work for your children, too.

After you have tried some of these lighter and medium range disciplines, you may need to move to heavier consequences if your children's hearts and behavior have not changed. As shown with David, he likely carried out some of these heavier consequences with his sheep, even having to break the legs of certain rebellious ones who were headed toward disaster.[9] This doesn't mean you should ever physically hurt your children in such a way; that would be terrible. Rather you may need to affect a heavier discipline when nothing else works.

There are at least two heavier measures that can be applied: spankings and separation. Spankings can be used when your children are young and separation when they are older. Both of these, though, drop into the category of last resort disciplines; they are not what you start out with.

The last resort of spanking

In respect to spanking, the general range suggested by many Christian family counselors and psychologists is between two and ten years of age.[10, 11] I stopped spanking in my progression around age seven.

There are a few exceptions to saving a spanking for a last resort, a child's safety or well being is one of them. When my son was very young he tended to wander off toward the street in front of our house, perhaps like one of David's sheep when straying to the outside of the trail on a dangerous mountain pass. In this situation with my son, I didn't follow a progression from lighter to heavier consequences; instead I sternly rebuked him and followed up with light spanking appropriate for his age. *(Proverbs 22:15)* Afterward, I hugged and told Brodie that I still loved him but reiterated that he would be spanked every time he ran toward the street. I did so because keeping him safe and alive was more important than a progression of discipline at this point in his life.

The last resort of separation

A second last resort of discipline is separation, which should only be used when your children reach the teenage years, probably high school and beyond. Hopefully, you'll never have to use this step, and likely won't if you build an intimate relationship and teach them the Scripture.

The discipline of separation involves sending an older child from the home because he or she has become too rebellious and unmanageable. The biblical idea and practice of separation comes from several instances in Scripture. Jesus' parable on the prodigal son is one of them. For the sake of reference here is a shortened version of the Prodigal parable as recorded by Luke.

And He said, "A man had two sons and the younger said to his father, 'Father, give me the share of the estate that falls to me.'" So he divided his wealth between them. And not many days later, the younger son gathered everything together and went on a journey into a distant country, and there he squandered his estate with loose living. But when he came to his senses, he said, "How many of my father's hired men have more than enough bread, but I am dying here with hunger! I will get up and go to my father, and will say to him, 'Father, I have sinned against heaven, and in your sight.'" So he got up and came to his father. But while he was still a long way off, his father saw him and felt compassion for him, and ran and embraced him and kissed him. And the son said to him, "Father, I have sinned against heaven and in your sight; I am no longer worthy to be called your son." But the father said to his slaves, "quickly bring out the best robe and put it on him, and put a ring on his hand and sandals on his feet." (Luke 15:11-13, 17-18, 20-22)

From an outside view, separating your son or daughter from the family looks like you don't care for them anymore. It even appears as though they are no longer a part of your family, but this couldn't be further from the truth. For, just as you are always a part of God's family after receiving Him as Lord, so too are your children always a part of yours no matter what they have done. When one of your children gets to the point where they are consistently disobedient though, you must take action. This may mean separating them from your family just as the father did in the Prodigal parable by letting his son go.

I have worked with a few families over the years that had to separate their teenage kids from their homes. One parent had to send her daughter to a lock-up situation in another state, while another handed her son over to a more discipline-oriented relative. Other parents chose military or boarding schools for their rebellious teenagers. All did because they loved their children and saw it as the only measure left to get their hearts changed. To my knowledge, most of them saw their kids make the turnarounds they hoped for, but it was not easy during the process.

The following are some guidelines which may help you determine whether your older children need to be separated from the home. I have also included some suggestions on dealing with them during their separation and return.

You should separate your older children when all other measures of discipline have been exhausted to no avail. You should also separate them if what they are doing is having a devastating impact on other members in the family, especially brothers and sisters.

If either or both of these are true, then get them to a place that can truly help them, preferably, a Christian program or facility if possible. While they are there, pray that they will repent of their sins and old ways just as the prodigal son did in Jesus' parable. Repentance made all the difference in the story for him; it will do the same for your son or daughter. Until your prodigal son or daughter has come to real repentance and sorrow for what they've done, they are not ready to come back home. This could take several days, weeks, and even months, so be patient. Meanwhile, carry on with your home as normally as you can. Dream good dreams about your prodigal, envision the day he or she will return with a changed heart. Imagine how God will use your son or daughter in the future. Take to heart that, as much as you want to see your prodigal come home changed, God wants this even more.

When they do return home with a changed heart, greet them with joy, just as Jesus portrayed the father doing in His parable. Be prepared and willing to help them out financially and in every other way. They won't come home without scars of hurt, perhaps only with a repentant heart. So, help them all you can and be patient with their recovery. In Jesus' prodigal parable, it was highly unlikely He saw the son coming home unscathed or unaffected by his circumstances. Jesus most likely viewed the prodigal son as starved, ragged, and beaten down by life. Therefore, strengthen your returning wayward one as the father did in Jesus' parable. If this means putting him or her in a rehabilitation center, special school, or just letting them rest at home for awhile, then do it. If you treat your returning children this way, your intimacy with them will not only be recovered, it will be made even stronger, as will your influence as you continue to teach them the Word.

Lastly, if they don't have a turn of heart and they continue in their rebellious ways, they can't come home. This may be incredibly difficult to do, but for their sake, and that of your family, you must not let them. Ask God for help with this, after all He knows first hand what you are experiencing and feeling. Think of all His children (mankind) over the centuries He couldn't let come home because they wouldn't repent and have a change of heart.

Final Thoughts

As you have seen, disciplining and correcting your children is a very important part in loving them. Without it, the Agape love God wants you to have with them cannot be fully realized.

In my experience with Tom, the little rebellious sixth grader in my class, my love for him at first had to be mostly expressed through discipline until his heart changed. In his story I briefly referred to my own sixth grade teacher, Mrs. Dean, who had done the same for me. I conclude therefore with her; without Mrs. Dean, and several others like her, I would never have received the discipline side of Agape love that I needed.

The first time I saw Mrs. Dean was the first day of school my sixth grade year. I was walking down the hallway when I caught site of her. She was waiting at the door of my classroom with arms folded. I had heard Mrs. Dean was tough, but I wasn't expecting her to look so serious and stern that first day.

As mentioned earlier, I came from a divorced home which left me without a father to discipline me when needed. Because of this, I ran rather wild for several years at Webster Elementary, causing disturbances in and out of the classroom. I broke just about every rule possible, got into fights, and showed little or no respect for authority. Amazingly, in the midst of all this, I had a relationship with Christ, whom I accepted as Lord and Savior before the divorce and family break up. Although, by my conduct at school, you would never know it.

The school administration was pretty frustrated with me, as I was sent to the office incident after incident. In fact I was so disobedient one year, I had to eat lunch in the school office for a time, but that didn't work long. I was so disruptive there that they sent me home to eat lunch until I got under control. This of course was very embarrassing to my mom who was a teacher at another school.

As a result, the administration at the end of my fifth grade year decided to shovel me off to Mrs. Dean, who was willing to take me on. In her preparation, she spent the entire summer praying for wisdom in how to deal with me. I know she did because she told me years later after I graduated from college.

When school started, she was ready to do what God had told her that summer. As I rambled down the hallway that first day of school, as confident as ever, there she stood at the door of the room with her arms folded. When I began to walk in, Mrs. Dean put her hand out to stop me and said, "Now, wait just a minute, Mr. McClain. Before you enter class, I am going to outline just what kind of year you're going to have in my class." And with that beginning, the year started. The first few days were a bit difficult because she was extremely tough on me. She never let me get out of control, never allowed me to do anything but my best in class, and she never stopped praying and caring for me. As the year went along, my heart started to change, and instead of fighting her, I began wanting to please her. Often, that is what loving discipline brings out. The principal's office was in awe, as I hadn't visited them once during the whole year, and I never got into another fight.

Now, you would think Mrs. Dean's responsibility was completed after I moved onto junior high. Not so, for she kept up with what I was doing, and continually prayed for me. Even when I went to high school, college, graduate school, and seminary, Mrs. Dean never lost contact nor stopped praying. Sad to say, she died a number of years ago, but I'm glad to say, she will never be forgotten for the loving discipline she gave me when I needed it most.

Teachable Moment

In my home garden, I have a number of healthy trees, but there is one fruit tree which has not produced consistently as it should. My gardener told me that if I left it alone, my orange tree would continue to bare less and less fruit each season. Eventually, it would produce nothing at all, hardly worth watering. I asked him to do whatever was necessary to make it healthy and productive again. As I watched him go to work, I was appalled at what he did. He began cutting away one branch after the next. I wondered if anything would be left when he was done. At first, he cut off all the ugly looking branches that obviously needed to be pruned. He then pruned all the succor branches that looked okay but had no ability to produce fruit. To my surprise, after a few months, this seemingly barren tree began to blossom, producing more oranges than ever before.

This garden illustration is a reminder of the importance of discipline in your children's lives. Like the gardener, you need to prune your children from the things they are doing that don't produce good Christian character. At first your rod of discipline may seem tough, hard, or even a bit drastic, but later on it will prove to be the right thing to have done. Therefore, every time you trim a flower, cut a blade of grass, or see a gardener pruning a tree, let it remind you that this is what you must also do with your children when they produce ugly branches and unneeded succors in their lives. They need your discipline just as much as my orange tree needed the gardener's pruning hands. With God's help and the assistance of His Word, you will be able to prune them well and eventually see the results. *(John 15:1-2)*

The following verses referenced in this chapter can be found in sequence on my web site, www.tmoments.com. Click on the Book Resources button located on the home page.

II Samuel 22:2-3; II Samuel 11:1-5, 13-14; Mark 4:37-40; Matthew 14:28-31; Jonah 3: 4-10; Deuteronomy 19:11-13; Galatians 6:7; Proverbs 22:15; John 15:1-2

TEN

THE STAFF OF GRACE, MERCY AND FORGIVENESS

(Applying needed grace)

Even though I walk through the valley of the shadow of death, I fear no evil, for You are with me; your... staff comforts me. (rbk)
(Psalm 23:4)

Shepherd with your staff, the children of your possession... [like] God who pardons our iniquities... and doesn't stay angry, but delights in an unchanging love toward us.
(Micah 7:14,18 [rbk])

As we have seen in David's shepherding, he often held two very visible tools of the trade in his hands for his sheep to see: a rod and a staff. In the previous chapter, the rod was used to depict discipline, just one side of the Agape love coin. In this chapter, the other side will be represented by the staff of grace, mercy, and forgiveness. To build intimacy with your children and teach them effectively, both sides of the coin will be needed.

The grace aspect of the staff is giving someone what they don't deserve; similar in principle to what Jesus did when giving all of us the unearned gift of salvation. *(Ephesians 2:8-9; Romans 3:10)* Mercy represents the suspended discipline or punishment we deserve, akin to the penalty God withheld from us due to our acceptance of His gift of salvation. *(Ephesians 2:4-5)* Lastly, forgiveness is the permanent pardon given after a genuine apology or repentance of a wrong-doing has been confessed. This is similar to the irreversible forgiveness God gives to all when turning from sin and believing in Christ as Savior. *(Hebrews 10:17-18)*

In arriving at a good basis for using grace, mercy, and forgiveness with your children, we will look at three statements David made about God in Psalm 23, "His staff comforts me," "He restores my soul," and "He anoints my head with oil." *(Psalm 23:4, 3, 5)* Then, we will view how Jesus applied His staff of grace, mercy, and forgiveness, particularly with Peter, Thomas, and other followers.

David

David depended greatly on his staff; it was just as critical to him as the rod. The staff was a wooden pole that stood five, six, or even eight feet tall with a crooked shape at the top. It looked like a giant question mark in the hand of a shepherd.[1] It had many functions, but perhaps one of the most important was to serve as a visible reminder to the sheep that the shepherd was near and would care for them if needed.[2]

Another function of the staff came when David used it to rescue his sheep from various dangers, including those resulting from poor choices, ignorance, or foolishness. When they fell either on or off the trail, many ended up on their backs. When this happened, they were incapable of righting themselves because of poor coordination and body weight. They helplessly stayed there with one stressful *bah* after the next until the shepherd came. When the shepherd arrived, he took the crook portion of his staff and hooked it around a part of the sheep's body and pulled on it until the sheep was up on its feet.[3] The hope of the shepherd in these incidents was that the sheep would "learn" from what they had done.

After such a rescue, David immediately mended his sheep's wounds until a more extensive restoring could take place in another location. There wasn't any discipline carried out during this time because it was designated for restoration. David refers to the mending he did with his sheep during these times in verses five and two of his Psalm 23, "*You anointed my head with oil... and restored my soul.*" Oil was the healing salve he used to take care of the sheep's wounds on the trail, but it was his loving strokes and encouraging words that took care of them in the green pasture.[4, 5] After an injured sheep had fully recovered, it took its place back in line with the others and continued on with the shepherd as if nothing had happened.

David's staff, his mending oil, and the restoring green pastures to which he led his sheep, show different measures of his grace, mercy, and forgiveness. To give his sheep more than they deserved demonstrated grace, particularly when rescuing them from bad situations they had gotten themselves into. Not penalizing them for making mistakes demonstrated mercy, especially during their recovery from injuries. Forgetting and not holding their blunders against them demonstrated forgiveness, as was the case when moving onto the next pasture without further rebuke or reproof. Each of these measures you will need to extend to your children if you want them to experience the staff side of Agape love.

Jesus

Jesus, like no other, knew how to use the staff of grace, mercy, and forgiveness as evidenced with His disciples and others, as well. He graciously gave Peter a key position of authority in the coming church, although he didn't deserve it. And Peter didn't; not many days after Jesus bestowed this great honor on him, Peter publicly denied Jesus at His trials. After Peter realized what he had done, He was filled with great sorrow and repented. In response, Jesus forgave him completely, and then gave him a full measure of His mercy. *(Matthew 16:18-19; Luke 22:61-62; John 21:15)* Accordingly, Peter's sins were forgotten, nothing was held against him, and no punishment was enacted. This is what you need to consider when using the staff of grace, mercy, and forgiveness with your children, particularly when they have demonstrated great sorrow for their wrong actions.

Jesus also demonstrated His staff of grace, mercy, and forgiveness with another disciple, Thomas. Even though Thomas demonstrated a tremendous lack of faith by doubting Jesus' resurrection, he was quickly forgiven and gracefully and mercifully restored after admitting his failure of unbelief. *(Matthew 28:16-20; John 20:26-28)* After Jesus' ascension, God used Thomas mightily as an ambassador to the world, particularly in the area of India as reported by several church historians.[6]

Jesus also used His staff of forgiveness with an adulterous woman brought before Him by the Pharisees who demanded that she be stoned according to the Law. Jesus refused to agree, but gave her mercy instead because of the repentance He must have seen in her heart. *(John 8:3-11)* Then there was the woman who washed His feet at the house of Simon the Pharisee, a woman full of immorality and past sins. He forgave her too because of her heart.

Turning toward the woman, He said to Simon, "Do you see this woman? I entered your house; you gave Me no water for My feet, but she has wet My feet with her tears and wiped them with her hair. You gave Me no kiss; but she, since the time I came in, has not ceased to kiss My feet. You did not anoint My head with oil, but she anointed My feet with perfume. For this reason I say to you, her sins, which are many, have been forgiven, for she loved much; but he who is forgiven little, loves little. Then He said to her, "Your sins have been forgiven." (Luke 7:44-48)

Parent Application

Here are some further thoughts to consider when applying grace, mercy, and forgiveness with your children, and are organized under the headings: *Permissive Parenting, Parenting with Grace, Parenting with Mercy, and Parenting with Forgiveness.*

Permissive Parenting

The staff of grace, mercy, and forgiveness is not a permissive, lax, or lenient side of Agape love. Permissive parenting is letting your children off-the-hook without consequences after they have been foolish, selfish, disobedient, or rebellious in their behavior.

Implementing the staff when working with your kids goes far beyond permissiveness because it asks something of them before grace, mercy, and forgiveness are extended. It asks for heart change, which usually includes a genuine apology (a desire to make things right) and/or repentance (a regret for doing wrong and commitment to change to do better).

Permissiveness, on the other hand, asks for nothing to receive grace, mercy, or forgiveness. There is merely the hope that by giving it, the heart and behavior of your children will change. There is no example or principle in Scripture that supports such an idea or practice. Some may argue that Jesus' gift of salvation was permissive in that sins are forgiven without us having to do anything in return. This is not true, for even though His gift of salvation is free and available to all, no one has ever been able to receive it unless they have demonstrated a heart change which only comes by repentance and belief. *(John 3:18; Mark 1:15)* Your children need to experience and demonstrate a similar kind of heart change to receive your grace, mercy, and forgiveness.

There are a few reasons why parents opt for permissive parenting, and none are very good. Some parents choose this route because it allows them to always appear as the so-called *good guy* with their children. They like being a hero to their kids, so they don't apply much discipline, nor do they ask or look for a heart change when giving grace, mercy, or forgiveness. Outwardly, these parents look very loving and accepting, but this is not so because they are not doing what is best for their children, just what's best for themselves.

Other parents who are permissive hope their acts of looking the other way will somehow be appreciated by their children; enough so to change their hearts and behavior. This view is unrealistic and also not supported in Scripture. If God had permissively acted this way toward us, whom He calls His children, then He would have taught and modeled it.

Parents may also use the permissive approach because they are either afraid of their own children or simply have not been taught how to use both sides of Agape love. These parents need to connect with and learn from those who know how to apply grace, mercy, and forgiveness without permissiveness.

Parenting with Grace

What does non-permissive parenting with grace entail? It means giving your children what they don't always deserve, but you do it anyway because of the heart change they have shown. In the story of Tom, I gave him a full measure of my grace the last week of school. I did so because he took the risk and decided to finally tell me the truth for the first time. He said, "Yes, Dr. McClain, I pushed a boy at recess which got us into a fight." In response, I gave him all the privileges the other kids had earned in my class. He was allowed to be a part of all the class parties and festivities. This was not something he deserved because his fight, according to school policy, should have grounded him. But because he demonstrated a heart change, I gave him grace as if he had done nothing wrong. If he hadn't told me the truth and I still let him off-the-hook, this would not have been grace but permissiveness.

In your parenting, you need to give grace to your children when they show genuine heart change. Just as David's sheep did with him, and he did with God when coming clean about his sins.

Be gracious to me, O God, according to Your lovingkindness; according to the greatness of Your compassion blot out my transgressions. Wash me thoroughly from my iniquity and cleanse me from my sin. For I know my transgressions, and my sin is ever before me. Against You, You only, I have sinned and done what is evil in Your sight, so that You are justified when You speak and blameless when You judge. (Psalm 51:1-4)

Finally, the grace given to your children should be decided ahead of time before they enter into the behavioral circumstances that might require it. You don't want your emotions or the *heat of the moment* to determine what you do in regard to grace. In this pre-planning of grace, it is not necessary to declare to your children what it will be. The father in Jesus' prodigal story didn't; the wayward son only found out about the level of his father's grace after he repented and came home *(Luke 15:11-13;17-21)* This is a good rule to follow with your children to keep them from acting repentant when they are not. Keeping your plan of grace undeclared may help them make a genuine decision of repentance which is what you want most.

Parenting with Mercy

Applying mercy, the second part of the staff, is not giving your children the disciplinary consequences they may have deserved. Once again as was the case with grace, the heart is the key. In some cases you will find that your children have suffered enough because of their actions. To discipline them further is unnecessary and can even be harmful. As seen with Peter, he certainly suffered enough after denying Jesus the way he did. The guilt he felt dramatically changed his heart. Therefore, it was quite unnecessary for Jesus to discipline him further; mercy was needed more. David did the same with his sheep as God did with him, for in both cases the resulting hurts from bad decisions and rebellious behavior was discipline enough.

Parenting with Forgiveness

Forgiveness, the third part of the staff, is giving your children a full pardon for what they have done. God expects you to forgive your children, no matter what, just as He has forgiven you for all your wrong doings. *(Mark 3:28; Ephesians 4:32)* In respect to this, here are four suggestions to mull over when forgiving your children.

1. Before forgiving your children, make sure their repentance is real, and this should be more than just a verbal apology. Often times, kids apologize just because they got caught and don't want to experience the consequences. A true apology is repentant in that the child is sorry for doing wrong and resolved to do right. Your children won't always master this perfectly and may relapse from time to time, but the question is, are they trying?
2. Once your children have truly apologized, repented, and have received forgiveness, discipline yourself not to keep bringing up their wrong doings; only talk about them if they want. Remember, Jesus

doesn't bring up the past wrongs of His disciples, neither should you with your children. Follow His example and you should be just fine in this area.

3. If your children do repeat a wrong and are repentant, act visibly surprised. Rather than saying, as too many parents do, "Here we go again, the same old you," say something like, "This is not you; you're better than this." And then remind them of what Paul said about being a new person in Christ.

Therefore if anyone is in Christ, he is a new creature; the old things passed away; behold, new things have come. (II Corinthians 5:17)

4. After you have forgiven your children, make sure your love doesn't decrease for them because of what they have done. If you find yourself doing this, then realize your love is becoming conditional which is not what the Lord wants. We know that Jesus had every right to love Peter less for denying him the way he did, but Jesus didn't; nothing ever changed His love for Peter, not even the worst of his actions. With God's help, neither should yours for your children.

Final thoughts

All three parts of the staff are intertwined with one another. When one is applied, the other two are usually involved in some way. If, for instance, you have given your children something they haven't earned or deserved (grace), then most likely you have also withheld a discipline or consequence (mercy). Where grace and mercy are present, it is almost impossible for forgiveness not to play a role. So in your application of the staff, don't try and separate grace, mercy, and forgiveness from each other, but let them flow together as they were intended to do.

In addition to this, carry out the full measure of Agape love with your children; it is vital that both sides, the rod of discipline and the staff of grace, mercy, and forgiveness, be done in a balanced and harmonizing way. If you are able to do this, the desired intimacy you should experience with your children can be realized. I've drawn from Scripture a four-step progression and written an article called *Balancing the Rod and the Staff* which is on my web site (www.tmoments.com). I invite you to read it when you get a chance. To summarize it, there are four sequential steps to follow when attempting to direct the heart of a child.

Step 1 – Apply the staff of grace, mercy, and forgiveness first, as God did with Abraham and Sarah when they sinned by refusing to trust Him for the child He had promised. (*Genesis 16:1-2, 4, 15-16; Genesis 17:18-21; Genesis 21:1-3*)

Step 2 – Let their hearts simmer for awhile in the grace, mercy, and forgiveness you have given them for a particular misbehavior. In a way, this is partially what God did with Israel after freeing them from their Egyptian bondage. During their forty years in the desert which followed, God gave them time to let their hearts cook in His grace, mercy, and forgiveness. What they should have received was immediate death for worshipping the golden calf. At the request of Moses, God didn't do this, but instead let their long trek through the desert change their hearts and minds so that when it came time to go into the Promised land they were ready. (*Acts 13:17-19; Exodus 32-33*)

Step 3 – Give a strong caution and clear warning of the consequences ahead if they don't show heart change and follow through. This is what God often did throughout the Bible with Israel, before disciplining them. His warnings to those under Solomon's care are just one example of this. (*I Kings 9:1, 3, 6-7*)

Step 4 – Exercise discipline as outlined in *The Rod of Discipline* chapter, matching what they did with your discipline, and moving from lighter to heavier consequences until their hearts have changed. (*Hebrews 12:5-7, 9-10*)

Achieving good balance between the rod of discipline and the staff of grace, mercy, and forgiveness eliminates a lot of guess work and mistakes when correcting your children. This four-step progression drawn from Scripture helps achieve this because it prevents overuse of either the rod or staff. Overuse of the rod can cause many problems with children; developing an unnatural fear of you is one of them. Overuse of the staff, on the other hand, can cause your children to lose respect for your leadership and authority in the home.

Teachable Moment

In the previous chapter, a garden was chosen to visualize the need for discipline in your children's lives. The pruning in that garden was analogous to the cutting away of those things that either hurt or didn't add to their growth or Christian character. The Teachable Moment for this chapter is the same garden, but this time viewed with the grace, mercy, and forgiveness you need to give your kids on a regular basis.

For a garden to thrive, pruning is important, but for it to survive, watering is essential. Without water and a consistent supply of it, a garden shrivels and dies, no matter how well pruned. So it is with your children who are each a part of your garden. If they are watered with your grace, mercy, and forgiveness they will not only survive but thrive, as well. Without it, they will likely wither away both emotionally and spiritually, that is unless God sends someone else to water them.

Therefore, the next time you water your garden, or see another's garden being watered, let it remind you of the great responsibility and call to give your children the grace, mercy, and forgiveness they need. You won't regret it, neither will your children.

And the Lord will continually guide you, and satisfy your desire in scorched places, and give strength to your bones; and you will be like a watered garden, and like a spring of water whose waters do not fail. (Isaiah 58:11)

The following verses referenced in this chapter can be found in sequence on my web site, www.tmoments.com. Click on the Book Resources button located on the home page.

Ephesians 2:8-9; Romans 3:10; Ephesians 2:4-5; Hebrews 10:17-18; Psalm 23:4, 3, 5; Matthew 16:18-19; Luke 22:61-62; John 21:15 Matthew 28:16-20; John 20:26-28; John 8:3-11; John 3:18; Mark 1:15; Luke 15:11-13; 17-21 Mark 3:28; Ephesians 4:32; Genesis 16:1-2, 4, 15-16 ; Genesis 17:18-21; Genesis 21:1-3; Acts 13:17-19; Exodus 32-33; I Kings 9: 1, 3,6-7; Hebrews 12:5-7, 9-10

SECTION III

The <u>P</u> in TIPS for Parenting

(Preparing your children to handle a fallen world and the future)

Instruct them to do good, to be rich in good works, to be generous and ready to share, storing up for themselves the treasure of a good foundation for the future, so that they may take hold of that which is life indeed.
(I Timothy 6:18-19)

This section is based on <u>514</u> verses in <u>193</u> different passages of Scripture.

Thoughts Ahead

100% means 100%, which means the Spirit can work just as much in your children as anyone else who trusts God.   Chapter 12

Abstaining from gossip, refusing to criticize your children's adult leaders in their extra-curricular activities, and not demanding that they get the best perceived teacher, demonstrate what the Christian should reflect.   Chapter 15

If you want your children to survive Satan's worldly influences, plan to do battle, either at his gates or yours.   Chapter 17

ELEVEN

DOMINIQUE

*(Preparing your children to handle a fallen world
and the future)*

*Therefore if anyone is in Christ, he is a new creature; the old things passed
away; behold, new things have come.*
(II Corinthians 5:17)

The following section is the third and final key to disciple your children. It is the P in the TIPS acronym, standing for the preparation your children need to handle a fallen world and the future ahead.

Your children were created and put on earth at this time for many reasons, but perhaps the greatest reason is to live out their faith before a world in desperate need of truth, morality, and salvation. And who knows, the way the world is going right now, perhaps your children's generation will be the last to be able to do this before Jesus returns, which makes your parenting role incredibly significant and important.

*For the Lord Himself will descend from heaven with a shout, with the voice of
the archangel and with the trumpet of God, and the dead in Christ will rise
first. Then we who are alive and remain will be caught up together with them in
the clouds to meet the Lord in the air, and so we shall always be with the Lord.*
(I Thessalonians 4:16-17)

Before giving you an overview of this section, I want to share with you a personal story about Dominique, another student in one of my sixth grade classes. I mention her because several things Dominique's parents did helped prepare her to deal with the challenges of this world, as well as the future ahead.

The Story of Dominique

It was the late spring of 1993, and all of my sixth graders were pretty anxious and excited about the coming history fair which was slated for the next day at school. In fact, the entire school was embroiled with similar projects at every grade level. During the course of the day, the projects were to be graded, and each class was allowed to walk through other classrooms to see what had been accomplished. To top it off, that evening was the school's official Open House when hundreds of parents, grandparents, aunts, uncles, brothers, and sisters were invited to come and see what each student and class had done. It was quite a big deal at our school, in some ways the highlight of the year. Without realizing it, competition had developed over the years at Open House between various classes and teachers.

I must admit that in the midst of preparing my class projects for Open House, I got caught up in the competition as well, especially this year. I did so because I was tired of being constantly surpassed by other teachers who seemed to be born with the ability to always create outstanding projects and extraordinary classrooms. So, I decided to do something about it, and instead of displaying my class's typical reports and projects on desks and bulletin boards, I had a brainstorm and went another direction.

At the time we were studying about Egypt. During the course of our study, we compared the afterlife beliefs of the Egyptians with that of early and present day Christians. The difference between the two beliefs was great in many respects, but it was the tombs of each that visibly expressed their greatest contrast. The tombs of the Egyptians, specifically those of the god-like Pharaohs, were impressive and larger than life. Many of them, like the Pyramids, still exist today. In contrast, the tombs of even the most noteworthy Christians of the day were mediocre, underground, and hidden from sight. Even Jesus' empty tomb was unimpressive, hardly what you'd expect for the Son of God. There was never a need for extravagant tombs for Christians, since the glory of what they did would be celebrated by God and His kingdom in heaven, not on earth.

In response to this unit on Ancient Egyptian history, I challenged my class to do something a little different for Open House. I told them we were going to build two tombs in our classroom, one dedicated to Pharaoh and the other to Christ. The class readily agreed and accepted the project without hesitation. Inside one tomb would be a mummy with the inscription, "Here lays Pharaoh, dead in his tomb, thought he was god, but was wrong." The other empty tomb would read, "Christ is not here, He has risen, He is in heaven, and so will you be if you believe."

Since we had about thirty students, I broke the class up into three different groups, building three pairs of tombs in all. The project ended up to be quite extensive, taking about a month to finish. Parents also got involved and came in on the weekends with their children to work on the tombs.

Needless to say, each group learned a lot about Egyptian and Christian beliefs during this time, but more importantly how to work with each other. However, there was one group that didn't do very well at first and a girl named Dominique was in that group. Before identifying the group's problem, and what was to be done about it, let me tell you a little about Dominique. She was one of my best girls in class, an 11 year old who had great character and was always conscientious about her studies. She came from a large family, all of whom loved the Lord. Her parents had a lot to do with this, for they were very dedicated Christians.

At the beginning of this project, her family underwent a very trying time as the father had a heart attack. On top of that he was a small business owner and the sole wage earner of the family; so without him working, the bills piled up. To make things even worse, he had very little health insurance which added even more bills to the pile. The entire family had to band together and cut back on expenses to help in anyway they could.

As the project got off the ground Dominique's faith was very strong, but as time passed things worsened with her father and so did her spirit. Nevertheless, she never missed an assignment or slacked off from doing her part on the project. I believe, in her way of thinking, this was the best way she could help her dad recover.

As the different projects developed, it eventually became clear that each student had to help buy needed materials, including those in Dominique's group. It wasn't clear what this cost might be, it was different for each group, but this was a moot point for Dominique because she had no money to give. When the money was collected, some girls began pressuring Dominique to pay, and weren't very patient or kind as they went about it. They didn't know what had been going on in her family; they just assumed she didn't want to pay her fair share. Seeing this trouble brewing, I waited until Dominique left the room for recess, and then I told the girls of her struggle. I took out some money from my wallet and paid for her part of the project. I then challenged the girls to be more compassionate with Dominique in the future and to remember that the Christian life is doing unto others as you would have them do unto you. The girls responded well, and thereafter showed the Christ-like compassion of which they were capable, the kind their parents had taught them.

Their project progressed very well after that and all in the group cooperated beautifully in getting things done. In fact, their tomb of Jesus was the most impressive of all, taking up one entire corner of the room.

The day of Open House finally came, and all my students arrived early to make their finishing touches. Of course, it was Dominique's hope to have her dad come that evening to see what she and her group had done, but that didn't seem possible. He was better but still very weak. When the evening began, everyone seemed drawn to our room, hundreds upon hundreds made their way through it, making some very nice comments about the tombs and the message that went with them. Even so, neither Dominique nor her family came. They decided that if their dad couldn't make it then they would all stay behind with him.

The next morning, I came in early to clean up. There was a lot to do, because the school had a policy to get all classrooms back together as soon as possible. As I made my way upstairs to my classroom, I saw Dominique and her dad about half way up. He was leaning on her for support. I quickly rushed to help him the rest of the way. In a cheerful, yet guarded voice, Dominique asked if she and her dad could have some time together in the room. "Of course," I said, "Take your time; we've got all day to clean things up," and then I left the room for awhile. When I made my way back a little later, I was just in time to catch them leaving. The father said to me, "I am very proud of my daughter, she has made my recovery so much easier." What a comment to make, a perfect comment!

It wasn't long after that Dominique shared in our class prayer time that her dad had made a complete recovery and was back at work. I believe if there is any passage of Scripture that fits Dominique's situation best, it is from the book of James.

Count it all joy my brethren when you encounter various trials and temptations, knowing that the testing of your faith produces endurance, and let endurance have its perfect result. (James 1:2-4)

The story gets even better. Our school sixth grade graduation, which was only a few months away, was also a big event. In addition to receiving diplomas and special awards, all five of our sixth grade classes performed a grand, speech-laden musical at graduation. Several of the sixth graders had instrumental solos, singing duets, and speaking parts. Over one thousand parents, grandparents, siblings, and family friends attended each year.

At the end of the evening, a special award was traditionally given to the student who demonstrated the best academics and Christian character during the course of the year. I was a part of the selection committee which included all of the sixth grade teachers. I think you can guess who I recommended for the award. Aside from my urgings, it was obvious to all that Dominique was the most deserving of this award, which aside from the honor, also included a free year of tuition.

In preparation for this musical production, Dominique was given an important speaking part by the director, Susanne, who was well aware of all that she had been through. The part was intended to be a reward for Dominique. The sixth graders practiced a great deal for this program, including every day the final week before graduation. On the last day, there was a final rehearsal just hours before the entourage of parents, grandparents, and family friends arrived. In the middle of this rehearsal, Dominique got very sick and couldn't continue. She had to be immediately replaced by another student. As you can imagine, Dominique was again sad and disappointed, perhaps wondering why the Lord could not at least reward her with this part for all she had gone through during the year.

As everyone took their places for the last rehearsal, Dominique sat despondently in the auditorium watching the one who took her place. I walked over to her and gently put my hands on her shoulders and said, "Don't be sad; the end of this day has not come yet." Of course she didn't know what I meant and was feeling too bad to ask. Regardless, I knew that at the end of the evening when her name was read to receive the special class award her feelings of disappointment would disappear.

After the rehearsal was over, Dominique went home and felt better. She returned that evening for graduation in good spirits along with her entire family. Her classmates started off the evening with the program they had been rehearsing, followed by a series of awards. The final award, the most important of all, the one she would receive, came after the diplomas were given out. Throughout the evening, I occasionally glanced over to see if there was any lingering disappointment on Dominique's face. There was none, not even when her part in the performance was done by another or when another student received an award that perhaps might have gone to her. Our teaching staff decided that I would be the one to give her the final award since she was in my class. I took the podium, explained the meaning of the award, and then with great joy, announced her name. It was a perfect end to the evening as far as I was concerned, but more so for Dominique. I believe it was like God saying to her, "Good job for the whole year, Dominique. You represented Me very well, good job my precious little girl."

As can be seen in this story, Dominique's parents did a good job of parenting. They prepared her well to handle difficulty which often comes through life in a fallen world. And from my understanding, they continued to prepare her for the future as well by building on some essential relationships which will be discussed throughout this section.

What's Ahead?

There are five relationships that are essential components to prepare your children for the world ahead. They include your children's relationship to God, the family, the church, school, and a fallen world.

Seven chapters are broken down into two separate parts to discuss these important relationships. The first part deals with your children's personal relationship with God, the importance of unity and togetherness in your home, the church's responsibility to your family, your family's relationship to the church, and your children's relationship to others at school. The second part deals solely with living in a fallen world permeated with temptation, distorted values, and evil.

The Biblical Examples

In this section the primary Scriptural references will be drawn from Paul the Apostle, Jesus, and the rest of the Trinity (Father and Spirit). Paul was chosen because of his incredible contribution to all areas of the Christian life, including those that can be applied to parenting. In fact, out of the 27 books in the New Testament, including the Gospels, Paul wrote about half of them.

Final Thoughts

In November of 2010, I had an opportunity to talk with Dominique almost 18 years after I had her in class. She was married and had four boys and a girl on the way. I was not surprised to see that her faith in God and resolve to raise her children according to the Scriptures were well in place. Here are a few of her own words after she read the account above.

"It's unbelievable how you recall the trials of my sixth grade year with such accurate detail. For me it is though it happened yesterday. Especially since that first heart attack, my father has had four more! The only thing I remember differently is that I arrived at graduation, but not recovered. I came even

though I had a 103 degree fever. I had pneumonia, but was not going to miss it! It was nice talking with you. I am glad to know you and your family are well and still on fire for the Lord. I wish you well with the completion of your book as it will definitely be one that I will be reading!!!

In Christ, Dominique"

TWELVE

100% OF HIM

(Your children's relationship with God)

*For God so loved the world that He gave His only begotten Son, that whoever
believes in Him shall not perish, but have eternal life.*
(John 3:16)

Out of all of the chapters in this section on preparing your children
for the world, this is the most important because it deals with their
relationship with God. Without a personal relationship with Him, your
children's other four relationships with the family, church, school, and
the world will end up hindered, misunderstood, or lost.

Having a personal relationship with God, guarantees your children
His constant presence, strength, wisdom, and unconditional love in the
years to come, no matter what befalls them. It is therefore vital in your
parenting that you do all that you can to make sure they end up with a
personal relationship with God.

In respect to this, some of Paul's fundamental teachings on salvation will
be discussed, specifically those dealing with God's grace and the response
of faith. Then, in regard to the importance of ministering to children, what
Jesus told His disciples at the height of His popularity will be recalled.

Paul

One of the many contributions Paul made to Christianity was how
clearly he expressed truth, especially in pursuing a personal relationship
with God and coming into His kingdom. Paul broke this teaching down
into three simple concepts, so that whether you are older or younger, you
could understand and apply it to your life.

The first concept was that salvation came by grace, and grace alone,
which in essence was God's decision to require nothing for salvation
except one's faith. According to grace, all good deeds, works, or merits
were insignificant, only faith in Jesus Christ the Son of God was critical.
This was because Jesus paid the price for the gift of grace by sacrificing
Himself on the cross. This one incredible act of His took care of all sin,
which opened the door for a relationship with God.

For by grace you have been saved through faith; and that not of yourselves, it is the gift of God, not as a result of works, so that no one may boast. (Ephesians 2:8-9)

"Blessed are those whose lawless deeds have been forgiven, and whose sins have been covered by the cross. Blessed is the man whose sin the Lord will not take into account." (Romans 4:7-8 [rbk])

But to each one of us grace was given according to the measure of Christ's gift." (Ephesians 4:7)

Paul's second concept was faith, which had two intertwining and dependent parts to it. The first was repentance, which involved being sorry for sin and admitting it before God. The other was belief, which was to put your trust in Christ, God's only provision for salvation. These two parts were never intended to be separated from one another. When one was done, the other naturally followed suit like two sides of a coin. This is because to repent means to turn away from sin toward God and to believe is turning to God and away from sin. This is perhaps why Paul, Jesus, and the other writers in the New Testament preached repentance on one occasion and belief on another, both meant the same. There were only a few passages where both were used together like Mark chapter 1 quoted below.

For the sorrow that is according to the will of God produces repentance without regret, leading to salvation, but the sorrow of the world produces death. (II Corinthians 7:10)

That if you confess with your mouth Jesus as Lord, and believe in your heart that God raised Him from the dead, you will be saved. (Romans 10:9)

Now after John had been taken into custody, Jesus came into Galilee, preaching the gospel of God, and saying, "The time is fulfilled, and the kingdom of God is at hand; repent and believe in the Gospel." (Mark 1:14-15)

The third concept of faith was reliance on God to get you through all the shortcomings and failures of this life, as well as into heaven one day. Paul made this point several times as indicated in his letters to the Hebrew Christians (assuming he wrote Hebrews) and to Timothy.

...for He Himself has said, "I will never desert you, nor will I ever forsake you", so that we confidently say, "The Lord is my helper, I will not be afraid. What will man do to me?" (Hebrews 13:5-6)

If we are faithless, He remains faithful, for He cannot deny Himself. (II Timothy 2:13)

Lastly, as you lead your children toward a relationship with God, read the Scriptures over and over again so that you can add to these three basic concepts that Paul emphasized. As you do, always remember that salvation is based on God's grace through faith. It's that simple!

Jesus

Most of Jesus' ministry was spent reaching out to adults, but this didn't mean He felt children weren't crucial to the kingdom. Children were very important to Jesus because they would carry on His words and messages to the next generation and establish His church. Therefore, as opportunities arose, Jesus spoke out for them with great passion. For instance, on one occasion at the height of His popularity when everyone was beckoning to see and hear Him, he openly scolded the disciples for trying to exclude children from having their time with Him too. *(Matthew 19:13-15; Luke 18:15)* As mentioned in chapter 5 Jesus valued children, and he informed the disciples and everyone else listening that the kingdom of God belonged just as much to children as anyone else, including even the smallest of them. He also added that the kind of pure and innocent faith children often exhibited was the kind He was looking for in others.

Thus, when deciding how much time and effort to spend bringing your children into a relationship with God, remember their spiritual lives are of the utmost importance to God. Shouldn't their spiritual lives also be of the utmost importance to you?

Parent Application

In addition to Paul and Jesus, there are other thoughts and guidelines to consider when leading your children to God, which are organized under the following headings: *Making Children a Priority and Presenting a Clear Message, Benefiting from Early Conversion,* and *Laying Children's Conversion in God's Hands.*

Making Children a Priority and Presenting a Clear Message

In the McClain home, introducing our children to a relationship with the Lord was a top priority. Due to this and a desire coming from the Lord, both Brodie and Shannon made commitments to Him when they were very young, around four and five years old.

In sharing the message of salvation with them, we did it gradually, teaching them only what they could grasp according to their age. After they got older and were able to think through concepts and beliefs, we asked them if they wanted to turn their lives over to Christ, and both said, "Yes." As we talked them through what to say and pray, we knew in the back of our minds that one day they would probably need to make this decision on their own, without the motivation of trying to please us. We rejoiced anyway when they said, "Yes," for who knows the heart of a child except God. Later on, after several years passed, both told us the commitment they made that day was real.

What we shared with them before praying to receive Christ was fairly simple and incorporated some of the basics Paul taught about salvation. First, in regards to God's grace, we told Brodie and Shannon that He loved them and wanted to have a forever relationship with them, no matter what they had done. We then explained God couldn't have this relationship because of something inside of them that needed to be taken care of. That something was sin, which caused them to be selfish and do the bad things they did. We then told Brodie and Shannon that they weren't the only ones with sin; everyone in the world had it too. To take care of it, they needed to do two things: Ask God to forgive them (repentance) and believe in Jesus Christ who died on the cross for all of theirs sins (faith). Lastly, we shared with our kids that when they did this (faith), then Jesus would come into their hearts and stay there forever, no matter what they did in the future, whether good or bad (grace again).

Later on, as the kids grew older and could understand deeper concepts, we explored in-depth God's grace (unmerited favor), faith (repentance and belief), the ministry of the Spirit, and staying right with God (sanctification).

Benefiting from Early Conversion

The earlier your children come to know Christ as Lord the better. It benefits them because they receive right away all the resources of God. One of the most significant resources is a full measure of the Spirit, who will guide, encourage, and empower them, even when they are young. (John 16:5-13; Acts 2:38) A full measure of the Spirit means they get 100% of Him, like everyone else who receives Christ. And **100% means 100%, which means the Spirit can work just as much in your children as anyone else who trusts God.** You might keep this in mind when working with them. Even though they may be very young or immature, this doesn't limit the Spirit's work in them, especially when they go through tough times.

This truth about the Spirit was critical to me while growing up. Without 100% of Him protecting, leading, and guiding me, I don't think I would have made it in life, at least not in respect to the things of the Lord. However, I did have the Spirit, because like my children, I accepted Christ as Lord and Savior when I was young.

I made this commitment at my dad's church at the conclusion of one of his sermons. He asked those in his congregation to come down to the altar if they truly wanted to make Jesus their Lord. I did, and without hesitation made my way to the altar to pray. My dad prayed with me and then asked if I knew what I was doing? I believe he wanted to make sure I was not just coming to the altar to please him. I assured him it was the Lord I was responding to and nothing else. He was relieved and then convinced.

Unfortunately, about a year-and-a-half later, as I shared earlier, my dad was tossed out of his church for immorality and my family broke up. In the midst of this mess though, I had 100% of the Spirit's presence, which got me through then and thereafter while growing up. One of the first things the Spirit put on my heart to do after receiving Christ was to pray. I did that every night before I went to bed, always reciting the Lord's Prayer at the end. I never missed a night, from six to 18 years old, after which I began shifting over to morning devotions.

So, don't put off making every effort to bring your children to Christ as soon as possible. In preparing them for the world, you never know what they or you will have to face in the future.

Laying Children's Conversion in God's Hands

As beneficial and important as it is to bring your children into a personal relationship with God when they are young, you still need to be wise and patient in the process. What you don't want to do is just give your children the words to say or concepts to agree to without them being understood or grasped in their hearts. Parents who do this often don't know what their children can grasp or they fear that if their children die before saying these things, they would go to hell and be lost forever.

Therefore, if you're not sure what your children can grasp, as I have reiterated through this book, get some advice and counsel. Ask questions of other successful Christian parents or Sunday school teachers who have worked with children like yours. Take a consensus of what you have heard before moving on with what to teach your children about salvation and their relationship with God.

And if you are worried about your kids dying before they get a chance to declare their faith, then relax; God is in control. Before your children were ever born, He had their hearts and souls in mind. According to the Scripture, it doesn't fit into His purpose or character to create children, judge them, and send them to hell before giving them a chance to respond in faith. Therefore, if they are too young to do this, then they fall under His grace and will be in heaven if they should die. Here are some Scriptures to support this, with attached comments.

For before the boy will know enough to refuse evil and choose good, the land whose two kings you dread will be forsaken. (Isaiah 7:16)

(An age of accountability is indicated in this verse. A child cannot be held accountable for what he/she doesn't know.)

The Lord is not slow about His promise, as some count slowness, but is patient toward you, not wishing for any to perish but for all to come to repentance. (II Peter 3:9)

(God desires that all of His creation be saved. Therefore it doesn't fit His desires to send children who have never had a chance to repent to hell.)

In the beginning was the Word, and the Word was with God, and the Word was God. And the Word [Jesus] became flesh, and dwelt among us, and we saw His glory, glory as of the only begotten from the Father, full of grace and truth. He was the true Light which, coming into the world, enlightens every man. (John 1:1, 14, 9 (rbk))

(God enlightens everyone of His creation to the truth. Therefore, if your children don't fully understand the words you want them to say, then realize God will get through to them as only He can.)

For You formed my inward parts; You wove me in my mother's womb. I will give thanks to You, for I am fearfully and wonderfully made; wonderful are Your works, Your eyes have seen my unformed substance; and in Your book were all written the days that were ordained for me, when as yet there was not one of them. (Psalm 139:13, 14, 16)

(God created all children out of love and gave them so many days to live here on earth. With this in mind, it doesn't make sense to reason that God created any just to throw them into hell without a chance to believe or experience His grace. It just doesn't fit the God of love He is.)

Final Thoughts

In the opening story about Dominique, the little 11-year-old girl in my class, she had two things going for her in the midst of her trials. She had parents who loved the Lord, and she had 100% of the Spirit due to a commitment she made to Christ earlier in her life. Such a combination was unbeatable for Dominique and will be for you and your children, too! So, stay with leading them toward Christ until you know they have made that decision for sure.

Teachable Moment

The importance of having a personal relationship with God is akin to certain elements of the sun. To illustrate this Teachable Moment compare the attributes of the sun to the presence of God. The sun, like God, is present everyday giving off light and warmth even in the worst conditions.

How often do you say during a storm that you hope the sun comes out soon? Yet in the midst of your waiting you realize the sun is always there and all that changes is the momentum of the storm. So it is with God in your life. He never moves from you after receiving Christ as Lord. All that moves are the stormy trials of life that come and go.

In regard to the light of the sun, let it remind you of God's truth (Bible). It can enlighten you with incredible perspectives every day, the same truth that led you to God in the first place. Finally, when you feel the rays of the sun on your face, let them remind you of the warmth of God's love. He will never withdraw His grace from you no matter what.

I give eternal life to them, and they will never perish; and no one will snatch them out of My hand. (John 10:28)

The following verses referenced in this chapter can be found in sequence on my web site, www.tmoments.com. Click on the Book Resources button located on the home page.

Matthew 19:13-15; Luke 18:15; John 16:5-13; Acts 2:38

THIRTEEN
TOGETHERNESS AND UNITY
(A child's relationship at home)

Behold, how good and how pleasant it is for brothers to dwell together in unity!

(Psalm 133:1)

The family relationship you provide for your children is another important component to prepare your children for the world and the future. This was somewhat alluded to in the Intimacy section which focused on the importance of building personal relationships with your children. This chapter speaks more specifically about how to sustain family togetherness and unity in a disruptive world.

There are several ingredients to accomplish this in your parenting, but three of the most important are displaying a humble heart, controlling inner-family criticism, and eliminating competition between your children. When these are handled well, your children will likely be well-equipped to handle whatever the world throws their way.

To establish a Scriptural basis to build and sustain family togetherness and unity, Paul's presumed childhood will be briefly constructed, along with what he taught about humility and criticism. After that, Jesus' surmised experience with His family will be discussed, in addition to two of His teachings dealing with authoritative leadership and rivalry.

Paul

The Scripture doesn't record a lot of particulars about Paul's family life; all we know is that through his various writings he had Jewish parents with Roman citizenship, a loving sister, and a dedicated nephew. The only specific passage addressing his family comes from the book of Acts, where his nephew saves his life. *(Acts 23:16-22)* According to circumstances surrounding this biblical account, Paul's beliefs and teachings enraged many Jews, enough so that 40 of them plotted against his life. In response, Paul's nephew warned him thereby saving his life. This doesn't prove his nephew and sister were believers, but it seems likely they were due to the risk taken on Paul's behalf. His parents were probably not. If they had been believers, it stands to reason Paul would have mentioned their faith somewhere in His writings. He certainly did with other parents who believed as seen with Eunice and Lois, the mother and grandmother of Timothy. *(II Timothy 1:5)*

Regardless of how much we actually know about Paul's family life, there are several teachings Paul gave that are pertinent to keeping a family unified and together. Two of these include serving others with a humble heart and controlling your comments and words.

Paul encouraged fellow believers to walk in a spirit of humility. To accomplish this, he felt believers needed to put others first, even above their own interests, needs, and wants. He also thought that those in authority should be open about their shortcomings, sensitive to others, and patient with those under their care. Here are just a few passages of Scripture that record Paul's thoughts, some you might take to heart when working with your own children at home.

Others first

Therefore if there is any encouragement in Christ, if there is any consolation of love, if there is any fellowship of the Spirit, if any affection and compassion, make my joy complete by being of the same mind, maintaining the same love, united in spirit, intent on one purpose. Do nothing from selfishness or empty conceit, but with humility of mind regard one another as more important than yourselves. Do not merely look out for your own personal interests, but also for the interests of others. (Philippians 2:1-4)

Open about shortcomings

It is a trustworthy statement, deserving full acceptance, that Christ Jesus came into the world to save sinners, among whom I am foremost of all. (I Timothy 1:15)

Not that I have already obtained it or have already become perfect, but I press on so that I may lay hold of that for which also I was laid hold of by Christ Jesus. Brethren, I do not regard myself as having laid hold of it yet; but one thing I do: forgetting what lies behind and reaching forward to what lies ahead, I press on toward the goal for the prize of the upward call of God in Christ Jesus. (Philippians 3:12-14)

Sensitive to others

> *Therefore I, the prisoner of the Lord, implore you to walk in a manner worthy of the calling with which you have been called, with all humility and gentleness, with patience, showing tolerance for one another in love, being diligent to preserve the unity of the Spirit in the bond of peace. (Ephesians 4:1-3)*

Paul felt managing critical comments was imperative and essential for family togetherness. According to him, such words often ended up unwholesome, graceless, and exasperating; particularly with children. This is something to keep in mind when making your home a "together-place" for your kids who, like you, can become targets of unkind and mean words from those in the world.

> *Let no unwholesome word proceed from your mouth, but only such a word as is good for edification according to the need of the moment, so that it will give grace to those who hear. Be kind to one another, tender-hearted, forgiving each other, just as God in Christ also has forgiven you. (Ephesians 4:29, 32)*

> *Fathers, do not exasperate your children, so that they will not lose heart. (Colossians 3: 21)*

Jesus

Scripture doesn't mention all of the particulars of Jesus' home life either, but more so than Paul's. We know, for example, who Jesus' earthly parents, his brothers, and sisters were. In respect to the accounts we have, it's reasonable to surmise that both Joseph and Mary were good parents. From the beginning Joseph demonstrated he was a man who loved, listened, and followed God's direction no matter the circumstance. *(Matthew 1:19-21, 24-25)* His acceptance of God's leading after the revelation of Mary's miraculous pregnancy was proof. Such a trusting response and quality surely dominated his fathering when taking care of Jesus as a child, as well as the other six children under his care.

Mary's mothering must also have been exceptional because she was strong spiritually and physically from the beginning. What mother, other than one sold out to God, could have withstood the ridicule endured when pregnant with Jesus? Further, what mother during the last week of pregnancy could have traveled 80 miles in the desert on a donkey to a place where Jesus was directed to be born? *(Luke 2:4-7)* Yet, Mary carried out these godly requests and, presumably, many more when raising her family. Finally, just as Mary was there for Jesus at the beginning and ending of His life on earth, so she would have been for each of her other children, because that was the kind of Godly mother she was. *(John 19:25-27)*

Jesus' siblings were born later to Joseph and Mary; James, Joseph, Simon and Judas were His brothers, but His sister's names we don't know. *(Matthew 13:55-56; Mark 6:2-3)* As a family, they were likely a very united one. The influence of Joseph, Mary, and Jesus assured this, as well as just being a typical Jewish family who revered the Scriptures and regularly attended synagogue. Even though Jesus' brothers and sisters didn't believe He was the Messiah until after the resurrection, they still followed and listened to Him. *(Acts 1:9-12, 14)* Most likely they did this because of their love for Him and the togetherness they developed as a family. *(John 7:3-5; Matthew 12:46-47)*

In addition to what can be gained from Jesus' family experience, what He taught about authority and the oversight of others is useful too, since this is a position that you as a parent hold with your children. What Jesus taught might surprise you. Aside from being Savior, Lord, and the Son of God, He was also a king; and not just any king, but the King of Kings and Lord of Lords. *(Revelation 17:14)* Though Jesus was a king, He identified His own authority and oversight of others as that of a shepherd. *(John 10: 11, 14)* A shepherd, as we saw earlier in the life of David, was dedicated to serving the needs of sheep, not the sheep meeting the needs of the shepherd. So it was with Jesus in His authority and oversight of others. He humbly served rather than demanding to be served. Not once in His entire ministry did Jesus lord His authority over others, but instead did things that kings or queens of His day would never have done, like washing another's feet or sacrificing his or her life for their subjects. However, this is exactly what Jesus did (and much more) because His authority was that of a shepherd who thought more of his sheep than Himself. This is what Jesus wanted His followers and leaders to do when overseeing others, to serve rather than be served. *(John 21:16; Acts 20:28)* This viewpoint is something to consider and take to heart when working with your own children.

...Whoever wishes to become great among you shall be your servant; and whoever wishes to be first among you shall be slave of all. For even the Son of

Man did not come to be served, but to serve. (Mark 10:43-45)

And He said to them, "The kings of the Gentiles lord it over them; and those who have authority over them are called Benefactors. But it is not this way with you, but the one who is the greatest among you must become like the youngest, and the leader like the servant." (Luke 22:25-26)

Therefore, I exhort the elders among you, as your fellow elder and witness of the sufferings of Christ... Shepherd the flock of God among you, exercising oversight... and not lording it over those allotted to your charge... (I Peter 5:1-3 [rbk])

Finally, what Jesus taught about competition is also helpful to you as a parent because most families struggle with sibling rivalries and even jealousies between children and parents. Unless this is dealt with effectively, your family may never experience the unity and togetherness it needs to combat a world reeking of envy, boasting, and competitive striving. *(Galatians 5:19-21)*

Throughout Jesus' ministry, He didn't appreciate it when the disciples argued with each other, especially when the topic was who would be the greatest amongst themselves. *(Matthew 20:21-28)* Jesus knew that if He didn't put a halt to such arguments, His disciples would become just like the very sinners they were trying to reach, full of dissention, hatred, self-love, and self-promotion. Therefore, after stopping them in their tracks, Jesus gave them a simple goal to follow, one that would take every bit of their faith to carry out. He told them to give in and serve one another. Instead of pursuing the greatest positions, they should go out and make others around them the greatest. This is something you must teach your children to do, so they won't compete and contend one against another.

An argument started among them as to which of them might be the greatest. But Jesus, knowing what they were thinking in their heart, took a child and stood him by His side, and said to them, "Whoever receives this child in My name receives Me, and whoever receives Me receives Him who sent Me; for the one who is least among all of you, this is the one who is great." (Luke 9:46-47)

Parent Application

The following are additional observations, expanded points, and applications to build family togetherness and unity. They are organized under the following: *Parenting with Humility, Managing Unloving Criticism,* and *Steering Clear of Family Competitiveness.*

Parenting with Humility

Parenting with humility is not easy for some parents, especially those who have grown up in homes where pride, criticism, and inner family competitiveness abounded. Regardless, humility must be a part of your parenting if your children are going to experience lasting unity and togetherness in your home.

Humility, according to a broad definition, means to revere, respect, and hold in high esteem the life of another.[1] In the Scriptures, humility is described as seeking another's needs and interests over your own, serving rather than demanding to be served, and the exact opposite of pride. *(Matthew 23:11-12; Mark 9:35)* As seen with Paul and Jesus, they espoused humility for the sake of bringing others into the kingdom, in addition to demonstrating how to live out the Christian life.

> *...Clothe yourselves with humility toward one another, for God is opposed to the proud, but gives grace to the humble. (I Peter 5:5)*

> *For you were called to freedom, brethren; only do not turn your freedom into an opportunity for the flesh, but through love serve one another. (Galatians 5:13)*

Achieving humility in parenting has several applications, which include shepherding with a servant's heart, willingness to admit mistakes, and adopting a "God-skin" with your children.

Shepherding with a servant heart

All parents have been given a position of authority over their children by God. In carrying out this responsibility, you need to be careful not to rule over and dominate your children. Shepherd them instead with a serving heart, the way Jesus did with His disciples, being willing to do the lowliest of tasks like washing their filthy feet.

Sad to say, some parents don't treat their children with much of a servant's heart. They instead choose to rule over them like royalty with subjects or slaves. This is too bad, as God did not give any parent the right to treat children this way. If you are in the habit of treating your children from the viewpoint of a king or queen, stop right away, repent, and start thinking of them as Jesus would…as young sheep to be shepherded, not subjects to be kept down.

Then He poured water into the basin, and began to wash the disciples' feet and to wipe them with the towel with which He was girded. (John 13: 5)

Be willing to admit mistakes

Parents who have humble hearts are not afraid to admit mistakes before their children and others when they have done something hurtful, wrong, or unfair. Therefore, if you do error, as we all do, then admit it to your children, even if it exposes some of your weaknesses or imperfections. Paul certainly did this with his followers; presenting himself as hardly perfect and even the worst of sinners.

Admitting your mistakes does two very good things: it builds an honest and forthright relationship with your children, and it shows them how to deal with their own mistakes and failures when they happen.

Adopting a "God-skin"

Parents with humble hearts are patient with their children, the way Jesus was with His disciples. No matter how many times they blew it, it never frazzled Him, nor caused Him to throw in the towel and look for others to disciple. In order to demonstrate such patience with your children, you should develop and maintain a God kind of skin with each of them. Often we hear the expression of having a thick or thin skin in regard to the actions of others. However, there is a "God-skin," too. It integrates the best qualities of both a thin and thick skin; a thin skin being sensitive, responsive, and compassionate, and a thick skin being unwavering, resilient, and disciplined. *(Ephesians 4:32; Hebrews 12:9-11)* Prayer, reading the Word, and looking to others who have good "God-skins" will help you develop one of your own over time. Just be patient with yourself, you will get one.

We urge you, brethren, admonish the unruly, encourage the fainthearted, help

the weak, be patient with everyone. (I Thessalonians 5:14)
The Lord's bond-servant must not be quarrelsome, but be kind to all, able to teach, patient when wronged. (II Timothy 2:24)

Managing Unloving Criticism

Effectively managing unloving criticism within your home is also an essential. This is not an easy task, because the world continually perpetuates and circulates this kind of criticism in almost every avenue of your family's life. It's played out on T.V. every night, at school, in the neighborhood, at your work place, and even at church. If you are not sure what unloving criticism is, please accept this simple definition: It is a combination of unloving comments not intended to correct another for their betterment, but rather to hurt, anger, discredit, embarrass, and/or exact revenge.

As you have probably already experienced in your own life, this kind of criticism didn't draw you closer to the ones giving it but, rather, farther away. In fact, it likely stirred within you a desire to criticize back, making your relationship with them even worse.

Thus, whatever you do, don't give way to using unloving criticism with your children. If you do, don't be surprised if they withdraw from you over time, as well as become divisive with one another. This kind of atmosphere in your home won't prepare them well for the world ahead, which is filled with this kind of criticism.

On the other hand, constructive criticism used in the right way, with the intent to help your children grow in their faith and personal maturity, can be a valuable tool and very much a family unifier, too. When employed this way, God and His Word stand behind you, because there is nothing wrong with correcting another as long as it is done with the right intent and in a loving way.

Correct your son and he will give you comfort. He will also delight your soul. (Proverbs 29:17)

The Bible seldom uses the word criticism, but it instead calls the process by other names like correction, rebuke, or reproof. *(Proverbs 27:5; Proverbs 15:32-33)* The only time criticism is used in the Scriptures is to describe the wrongful judging of another, as recorded in James 2:4. Therefore, in respect to this, perhaps it might be best to throw out the term criticism altogether when talking about correcting your children for their own good.

Regardless of whether you throw out criticism as a term or not, its misuse must be monitored carefully in your home. As Paul suggested, don't frustrate your children by throwing negative remarks at them when they don't live up to your expectations or do what you want. However, don't hesitate to tell your children they have done wrong when they have, just follow up with ways to change and improve. If they refuse, use the principles laid out in the previous chapters on applying the staff of grace and rod of discipline.

Finally, if you want to make sure your family experiences the full measure of the togetherness and unity God intends, start by showing them how to rightly receive correction, rebuke, and reproof when it comes your way. Your example in doing this speaks the loudest; for as you do, so will they. As many times as you can, encourage your children to be like ducks in water when it comes to receiving unloving criticism; teach them to let it roll off their backs. If need be, say "quack, quack" to remind them of this.

Steering Clear of Family Competitiveness

Another important step in maintaining togetherness and unity is steering clear of family competitiveness. Even if you think pitting your children against one another will bring out their best qualities or efforts, don't do it! It's not worth the possibility of creating ill feelings between them.

Pitting one against the other is often promoted in competitive sports but should not be used to build a family relationship. I made this error early in my parenting, because much of my extracurricular life was spent either playing or coaching sports. Influenced by this, I thought I could get the most out of my son and daughter by getting them to compete against one another. At first, I got some okay results, but as time wore on, I could see they were developing a distance between one another. Instead of loving and supporting each other, they vied for who would be best, whether in sports, academics, or just playing checkers. Fortunately, because of my wife's persistent influence, I abandoned this approach. In its place, I followed her example and began encouraging Brodie and Shannon to be each other's biggest cheerleader instead of competitor. It took only a little time to make this transition, but our family togetherness and unity greatly improved. I will never forget all of the games Shannon attended just to root for her brother or the great sacrifice she made when giving up a state track meet to be at her brother's college graduation. Brodie did much the same for Shannon attending her games when possible, even while in college.

As seen in Jesus' discipleship, He demonstrated the importance of quickly quelling competitive battles. His purpose was to build humility, togetherness, and a genuine love amongst His disciples. You need to do the same with your children, which may mean getting them to sacrifice their own needs for others in the family. When they do, applaud and praise them each time for doing so.

Final Thoughts

In the opening story of Dominique, both criticism and competitiveness were played out, but in good ways. In respect to criticism, I rebuked a couple of girls in Dominique's group because they showed great insensitivity toward her when she couldn't pay for her part of the Open House project. If I had just been content to leave them with a criticism, then I would have only vented my disappointment or disgust and nothing more. Dominique would have continued to be hurt, and the two girls would have learned nothing about class togetherness and relationships with one another. However, with a rebuke (a term I substitute for criticism when loving correction is in mind), I followed up with a plan for them to change what they did. The girls responded well, making things right with Dominique, and even going a step further by being more sensitive toward others in class. Because of this, we all bonded together like a loving family.

On the last day of school, many cried instead of cheering when the final bell rang. I believe they did because they realized they would never be together again as a class and that was heartbreaking for many, even some of the boys. I pray your family will have the same experience and even greater feelings toward each other when your kids finally leave the roost.

In respect to competitiveness, I was impressed with Dominique's family at graduation. She had many brothers and sisters with the potential to compete against one another as many families end up doing. Yet, at her graduation, each eagerly watched Dominique walk across the graduation stage with great joy. I know because I watched them the entire evening, as well as many other times during the course of the year. When she won the top award, you would have thought her brothers and sisters had all won it; they were so excited for her! Competitiveness evidently was not a part of Dominique's relationship with them and their praise for her that evening demonstrated this. Eliminating it in your family may get you the same results, even more so, who knows?

Teachable Moments

To remember the main thrust of this chapter, try duplicating Jesus' washing of His disciple's feet. If your children are old enough to participate, I would do it the following way.

I would first ask the kids to play outside with their sandals on, weather permitting. The purpose is to get their feet dirty, like those in Jesus' day who only had sandals to wear for shoes. After awhile, I would have each come in and clean the feet of another. Afterward read the story of Jesus' washing of His disciple's feet as recorded in John 13:5-15.

At the end of the reading, highlight Jesus' humble servant's heart to do even the lowest of duties for His disciples, just as each in your family should consider doing for each other when possible. List some of those possible lowly duties, so they can have an idea of what to do when opportunities arise to serve each other. Such a practice will no doubt build on and sustain the level of togetherness and unity your family will need in order to face the challenges of this world.

Finally, label the dirt washed away in this illustration as the unloving criticisms and self- promoting competitions that may need to be cleaned up between each of you. Cleaning the dirt off begins by saying, "I'm sorry, please forgive me."

The following verses referenced in this chapter can be found in sequence on my web site, www.tmoments.com. Click on the Book Resources button located on the home page.

Acts 23:16-22; II Timothy 1:5; Matthew 1:19-21, 24-25; Luke 2:4-7; John 19:25-27; Matthew 13:55-56; Mark 6:2-3; Acts 1:9-12, 14; John 7:3-5; Matthew 12:46-47; Revelation 17:14; John 10:11, 14; John 21:16; Acts 20:28; Galatians 5:19-21; Matthew 20:21-28; Matthew 23:11-12; Mark 9:35; Ephesians 4:32; Hebrews 12:9-11; Proverbs 27:5; Proverbs 15:32; James 2:4; John 13: 5-15

FOURTEEN

GIVING BACK TO THE CHURCH YOU CHOOSE

(A family's relationship with the Church)

But in case I am delayed, I write so that you will know how one ought to conduct himself in the household of God, which is the church of the living God, the pillar and support of the truth.
(I Timothy 3:15)

...And remember the words of the Lord Jesus, that He Himself said, "It is more blessed to give than to receive."
(Acts 20:35)

A third important relationship that helps prepare your children for the world ahead concerns the church, one of the most vital connections you will need to help you in parenting. The church is important because it is God's families on earth, made up of other Christian parents just like you who are trying to raise their kids to love God and maintain good standards and morals.

This chapter, therefore, deals with the make up of a good church and how your family should respond to it. As is true with any good relationship, whether it is between a husband and wife or children and their parents, it takes a lot of giving and receiving to make it work. The church needs to give to your family, and you and your children need to give back in return.

To build a basis of what makes a good church for your family, the terms and language Paul and Jesus used describing fellow believers will be discussed. In addition to this, Jesus' approach to teaching the Word will again be referenced, since this is one of the main duties of a church.

Paul

In many of Paul's writings, he encouraged those in the early church to minister to each other like a family. In his Epistles, he called fellow believers brothers and sisters in the Lord and referred to the entire church as the household of God. *(I Corinthians 9:5; Romans 16:1; Galatians 6:10; Ephesians 2:19)*

Paul also stipulated that all potential candidates for leadership should be able to handle their families well. *(I Timothy 3:2, 4, 5)* He taught this for two reasons, the first being that he wanted church families to be good examples for others to follow. Secondly, Paul desired that the early church be handled like a close-knit family. Contrary to today, Paul was not consumed with budgets, facility concerns, or the building of large church plants. His focus, like the other disciples, was solely to disciple, teach, and equip the family of God so they could become great examples of Christ to the world. Therefore, when considering a church, you need to make sure the church you choose acts like a family and has leaders whose families are doing well spiritually. If it doesn't, how can your church teach you how to do so with your family?

Finally, Paul was a great example of one who gave back to the church, far more than he received. When he moved onto another church, it was usually to bolster its members in their knowledge of God and faith, not because he was looking for something better. And when he left a church, he never forgot those with whom he spent time, often writing them about their concerns and problems. In his faith experience, there was no such thing as an out-of-sight, out-of-mind perspective when it came to other believers. You should remember this if your family moves onto another church. Just because your old church is no longer meeting your family's needs as it once did, doesn't mean you can't try to meet some of its needs. You do that by keeping in contact and praying for those you once had in close fellowship.

I thank my God in all my remembrance of you, always offering prayer with joy in my every prayer for you all, in view of your participation in the gospel from the first day until now. (Philippians 1:3-5)

Jesus

Jesus also called His followers children, sons, daughters, brothers and sisters, and referred to the church as the household of God. He could have referred to them differently, perhaps as congregants, attenders, parishioners, clients, or customers, but didn't. Instead, He looked upon each as members of His family, who He loved and to whom He deeply wanted to reach and relate.

"For whoever does the will of God, he is My brother and sister and mother."
(Mark 3:35)

"But I have prayed for you, that your faith may not fail; and you, when once
you have turned again, strengthen your brothers." (Luke 22:32)

When Jesus met with those He called brothers and sisters, He did so in the humblest of places, such as an open field, a mountain ridge, the edge of a lake, or the confines of a small synagogue. *(Matthew 13:53-54; Matthew 5:1-2; Luke 5:1)* Very few times did He teach in a big formal arena, like the Temple in Jerusalem. It just wasn't the place where the level of intimate discipleship He wanted for His followers could be accomplished.

When Jesus taught, a responsibility all churches should carry out with their families, He used a variety of parables, illustrations, and Teachable Moment type of communications to convey His points. And as He taught, Jesus proclaimed the whole counsel of Scripture, covering just about every theological subject and life situation. He also didn't exclusively employ a particularly positive or negative approach in His preaching. Sometimes He encouraged, gave hope, and built up His followers, while at other times he rebuked, admonished and warned them. *(Matthew 5:2-9; Luke 8:24-25; Matthew 19:13-14)* Consider this approach when looking at what your church should be doing to help your family with the challenges of this world.

Parent Application

In the following applications there is a two fold emphasis; the first describes attributes required in a church to best meet the needs of a family, and the second delineates what a family needs to give back to the church. The following applications are organized under two main headings with several sub-points: *Considering the Best Church for Your Family,* and *Giving Back to Your Church.*

Considering the Best Church for Your Family

You may be attending a church where you are content and happy because most of your needs as a family are being met. If so, then take the following church considerations and applaud your church leadership for the good work they have done. This will not only encourage them, but it will keep them on track to continue doing what they have done for your family. If your church is not doing some, or many of the things listed below, bring it to their attention, but with a willingness to get in and help them where possible. Here are some qualities, traits, and characteristics to look for in a church and those to avoid.

Churches that center on children's ministries

Consider a church that focuses on the needs of children. Such a church would most likely have a well developed and thought out Sunday school curriculum, as well as a midweek program like Awana. The volunteer teachers and helpers who make up the Sunday school staff should be experienced or skilled in working with children of all ages. In your parenting, you may need their expertise. Children are not little adults as some parents assume; they are kids and understand things as kids. *(I Corinthians 3:1-2; Hebrews 5:12-14)* Sunday school teachers and workers know this and work with them accordingly. Aside from teaching the great truths of the Scripture according to what your children can grasp and understand, Sunday school teachers and workers can also help you teach your own children at home. All you have to do is observe how they communicate to your children at church and then emulate this at home. It is that simple. A church that dedicates itself to such an emphasis with children can help you a great deal in making your kids equipped to handle the challenges of this world.

Churches that teach God's Word

Consider a church that consistently preaches and teaches God's Word from the pulpit week after week. The wisdom you can gain as an adult from such teaching is not only helpful for your own spiritual growth, it is vital for your children's, too. Whether you realize it or not, what you learn about God's Word will continually transfer over to your children. From the outset of their lives, they want to know everything you know about the world in which they live, how it works, what to expect, what is true, and what is not. They look to you first for answers, so it is important you give them God's perspective from the *get go*. The wisdom both you and they will grasp from the Scripture is unmatched by anything the world can offer. The most amazing thing about God's Word is that it has an ability to effectively teach the same truth to all ages. Therefore, choose a church that dedicates consistent time to regularly preaching the inspired and inerrant Word of God. Particularly a church that teaches the whole counsel of Scripture, with a variety of vivid and memorable illustrations as Jesus did with His disciples. *(II Timothy 3:16-17)*

Avoid those churches that don't do this, because sermons that are not based on the Bible can lead to skewed thinking and false assumptions. Such could not only hurt your walk with God, it may hurt your children's, too. If you have to choose between a church that consistently teaches the inspired Word and one that doesn't but has a great children's program, I would choose the first one. The value of a child knowing God's truth as it was intended to be taught outweighs and outlasts any children's or youth programs, no matter how good they might appear.

Churches that give good parenting counsel

There are a slew of good parenting books on the market to read, and I would suggest reading some of them. However, I believe the best counsel comes from other Christian parents who are raising children like you. A church filled with successful parents and grandparents can be more valuable then any other resource. I believe Dominique, the girl in the opening story, was a part of a church where there were many Christian parents helping each other with timely advice and counsel. Therefore, consider a church that has a solid core of mature Christian parents from which to draw wisdom. Paul somewhat alluded to the importance of having mature parents in a church body when he made it one of his qualifications for church leadership.

It is a trustworthy statement: if any man aspires to the office of overseer, it is a fine work he desires to do. He must be one who manages his own household well, keeping his children under control with all dignity. But if a man does not know how to manage his own household, how will he take care of the church of God? (1 Timothy 3:1, 4-5)

Churches that create opportunities to serve

Consider a church that creates opportunities for your entire family to use their gifts and abilities. Part of God's call to every believer is to serve within the church in one capacity or another. As Paul stated, each believer is given at least one spiritual gift to help accomplish the ministry of the church.

Since we have gifts that differ according to the grace given to us, each of us is to exercise them accordingly: if prophecy, according to the proportion of his faith; if service, in his serving; or he who teaches, in his teaching. (Romans 12:6-7)

This is especially important for your children, who need to learn early that they should give to the church as much as take from it. You are their best example in grasping this service concept; if they see you serve, then they will likely follow suit and do the same one day. Better yet, if you can serve together with them in a particular ministry, they can learn directly from you how to do it. This is very much how Jesus worked with His own disciples. He not only taught them the Word, He showed them how to minister by doing it with them.

Years ago when I was in charge of the ushers at church, I often teamed sons and dads together on certain Sundays to seat members and attendees and take the offering. The whole idea was to give the sons a sense of service, and what better way than to do it with dad. Later on, we included daughters with their dads and it was always well received. I believe today that many of those sons and daughters faithfully serve as young adults in churches they are attending, all because they learned how to serve the church with their dads. Find a church that encourages such service for your whole family. If you are in a good church that has yet to grasp this, approach the leadership to do so. I am sure they would be thrilled to have your whole family help meet the needs of the church through your service.

Other ways your children can use and develop their gifts and abilities in church as they grow older is to be a part of a youth program that has serving others as one of its purposes. I was a part of one in my church when I was young, and it made all the difference in the world for me. Sonny Salsbury was my youth director, and he saw early on that young people needed more than just a weekly dose of Scripture on Sunday mornings. They also needed experience to go with it, similar in principle to the opportunities Jesus gave His disciples. He used his own gifts of music, teaching, and leadership to do so and made his youth group into a traveling choir of sorts. I say "of sorts," because we were not like the typical 60s church youth choir of our day in that we had guitars, drums, ukuleles, base instruments, and were a bit rock and roll at times in our approach. And whether we were singing in a church, hiking in Yosemite, or simply sharing the Gospel with hippies on Haight-Ashbury Street in San Francisco, we were all growing in our knowledge of the Word, in our abilities to serve Him in our various ways, and in our social relationships with each other. Whereas most of our other friends were struggling with the temptations of sex, drugs, alcohol, and even church legalism, we were too busy to do so. In the end, each of us developed a love for each other that was wholesome, good, and still lasts to this day. Just last year we had a reunion where we watched a video and pictures of ourselves together during those early 60s. Thus, it is important for your children to have a church that not only gives young people opportunities to serve but opportunities to do wholesome and lasting activities with other Christians their age.

Churches that promote balance

Consider churches that promote good balance, ones that not only establish areas of service for your family, but don't go overboard in asking too much from you. Such churches are wise enough to know your family has a life outside of them which is also important to God. I once had a situation where I was in charge of the Christian school at a church. One of our school board members was a dedicated family man, a valued employee at work, and a great church member who served in several capacities. After about a year on our board, I asked him to step down. It wasn't because he was a slacker or lacked in any quality, but quite the opposite. He was just doing too much! His family, neighborhood, and work needed him, too! He reluctantly stepped down, but I think it was for the better. I can't say as a church leader that I always followed this path with others at church because I, like many other pastors, sometimes asked too much from my members. So, pursue a church that wants you and creates ways for you to serve, but one that also recognizes you and your children have other ministry obligations outside of it. If you are in a church that is asking too much, then explain the situation and respectfully resign some of your duties.

Avoid churches that hurt families

Some churches have traits, qualities, and ways of doing things that, sad to say, can also hurt families. They usually do so because of three main reasons: ignorance, self-interest, and guilt trips. If you are looking for a church, avoid churches like these, and if you are in one but don't want to leave, then ask God to help you encourage them to make the necessary changes.

Churches can hurt your family when they treat you like a part of an organization, rather than a family. They frequently do this when growth occurs because they don't know how to handle it. In their excitement of swelling crowds, they change their ministry from family orientation to a business. Instead of the church being the household of God as Paul and Jesus taught, they are now a church company in the business of attracting as many customers and clients as possible. In the midst of their ignorance, the leadership core switches from being shepherds to general managers over their people. Eventually, their leadership meetings are consumed with business matters, staff procedures, productivity discussions, facility operations, and new building needs.

Certain large churches can also hurt families, especially churches intentionally seeking growth for their own glory and not God's. *(John 7:18; John 12:43)* Churches who seek their own glory are usually overly engaged in a number of wrong pursuits. They often, for instance, do any and everything to attract crowds. There is not a program they will not introduce for the sake of gaining new members. Consequently, they gather more people than they can possibly manage, disciple, or shepherd, but they don't care. They love the glory of being big. In addition to their pursuit of numbers, they also ask for more and more contributions to reach their goals, sometimes far beyond what people can bear. In their eyes, upgraded facilities, added professional staff, and new buildings are far more important than helping the hurting, meeting the discipleship needs of their people, or supporting missions.

Their preaching can also become skewed as they don't want to say anything that might turn someone away, especially during a building campaign. Instead of teaching the Bible as written, they emphasize only the positive and affirming parts, rather than the whole counsel, which includes warnings, rebukes, and consequences. *(II Timothy 4:2-3; Acts 2:27)*

If Jesus had spent His time building this kind of a church, He would have most likely set up shop in Jerusalem to draw bigger crowds. He would have used the impressive Temple as His pulpit and spoken only to large crowds once or twice a week on subjects they wanted to hear.

Instead, Jesus chose humble surroundings from which to preach, and often spoke just as much to a few as He did to the crowds seeking Him. (John 4:9-10; Matthew 5:1-2) He also taught what the people needed to hear, rather than what they wanted to hear.

Avoid guilt producing churches

Be cautious and wary of churches that constantly put guilt trips on their members, for it may negatively impact your children in the years to come. (Matthew 23:2-4) Children who grow up in guilt-ridden churches often reject church all together when they become adults. Once again, it's important for a church and its pastors to teach the whole counsel of God, which includes the joyous and affirming parts of God's grace taught throughout the Bible.

> Therefore, having been justified by faith, we have peace with God through our Lord Jesus Christ, through whom also we have obtained our introduction by faith into this grace in which we stand; and we exult in hope of the glory of God. (Romans 5:1-2)

> It was for freedom that Christ set us free; therefore keep standing firm and do not be subject again to a yoke of slavery. (Galatians 5:1)

The pastor in a guilt-oriented church often makes his members feel ashamed for not living up to certain church standards, which may or may not be biblically based. His sermon applications are more often than not centered on what you have not done to please God. Pastors and leaders who dish out such guilt can really hurt your family as they end up demanding more from you than God does. They also see your time at home, or with other pursuits outside of the church, as a rival.

Consider small churches

Finally, small churches can be a good option for your children. In this setting they can receive special attention and care from everyone in the congregation, including the head pastor and others in leadership. According to some recent statistics, the medium size for a church in the United States is 75 members; so there are plenty from which to choose.[1]

Children of all ages need special attention now more than ever, because they are growing up in a culture that is gradually losing touch with basic goodness and Christian morality. Therefore, if you are in a church where that special attention cannot be given to your children, consider a smaller church. It is better they miss out on the children's programs larger churches offer than to be lost in the crowd, where the leadership have no idea who or where they are spiritually.

Giving Back to Your Church

Being a part of a church that will help your children grow spiritually and be prepared for the world ahead is not just receiving what a church can give but is also giving back to it. In respect to this, there are two thoughts to consider: What happens when families give back to the church, and What happens when families don't.

What happens when families give back to the church

Assuming you have settled into a good church that gives a lot to your family, what should you give in return? Is attending a weekly service, sending your children to the Sunday school, and giving of your tithes and offerings enough? With few exceptions, most likely not, especially if you compare this to what earlier generations of Christians did for the church. Had it not been for these early Christians and their willingness to give of their time to the church, who knows what kind of a spiritual state we would be in today. However, they did, and we are still enjoying the fruits of their labors.

Every church in every generation is given a mission and ministry by God to achieve. Everyone in every church, including parents with children, is given a responsibility in that mission and ministry. No one is designated just to be served, but all are called to serve. *(Galatians 5:13)* In respect to families, there is a twofold ministry that can be experienced, one which helps the church in the here and now and the other in its future. Here is how this works: when your children observe or help you accomplish a task or role at church, it immediately impacts the ability of the church to accomplish its current ministry. But it also helps the church for the future, because your children, who have learned how to do ministry by watching and participating with you, will be the ones most qualified to lead it in the years to come. This is very much like what happened with the children of families in the early church who were equipped to lead the church during the next generation.

Thus, look for opportunities to serve in your church. If you can, choose a church that involves the whole family, as this could very well provide a natural setting for you to disciple your children. Parents who serve as Sunday school teachers not only help fill an important church need, they also show their children how to teach God's Word and manage a classroom. However, if you can't be in such a role at church, at least let them see you in a spiritual leadership responsibility, which they will most likely want to emulate one day.

When I was a children's/family life pastor at a large church in Arizona a number of years ago, I saw several parents volunteer to be their own children's Sunday school teacher. I was very much impressed with them to say the least. Yet, some even took it a step further and volunteered to teach younger aged classes so their own children could assist them in the teaching, which in my thinking was a superb display of discipleship.

Now, if teaching is not your gift or forte, assist other Sunday school teachers or team up with your children in other church ministries. One such ministry could be in greeting new people who come to church. This is a very important ministry and every church should have it. Many times visitors will return if they are cordially welcomed, particularly by loving and enthusiastic children. I was in charge of such a ministry once that needed over 30 greeters every week. In order to do this, I enlisted entire families to help, which included fathers, mothers, sons, daughters, and even grandparents. It turned out well; visitors returned, but more importantly, the families who participated got a chance to minister together.

There are other ministries where discipleship between parent and child can take place in the church, such as Awana, Pioneer Clubs, and other children's programs. The important thing is for your entire family to give back to the church just as Jesus, Paul, and other Christian families did throughout the centuries.

What happens when families don't give back

What happens when families don't give back and all they do is take from the church for their own purposes? The answer is simple, the work of the church and the spread of the Gospel suffers. It does because others in the church have to do all the work that needs to be done. When too many families in a church do this to others, then those picking up the slack eventually *burn out*. This usually leads to ending certain ministries that might have made an incredible difference in the years to come had they been able to keep going.

Amazingly, families who don't give back don't seem to care about this as long as their needs are being met, and that's sad. It's sad because the church needs them; it's sad for God who created them to do good works; and it's sad for them because they are missing out on some great opportunities to make a difference for the kingdom of God.

For we are His workmanship, created in Christ Jesus for good works, which God prepared beforehand so that we would walk in them. (Ephesians 2:10)

Some families I encountered over the years in ministry who refused to give back had some very selfish reasons. Some left for other churches when asked to help, feeling it was the church's job to teach their children. Other parents dropped their kids off at Sunday school while going to the nearby mall to shop. Still other mothers and fathers picked their kids up late from Sunday school every week, not because the sermon went a little long, but because the time it took for their errand runs got away from them. I could go on and on with similar situations, but the point is that the church suffers when families don't give back as they should. Please don't be a family that doesn't give back; it won't help you prepare your children for the world.

Final thoughts

If you should ever consider leaving your church for another because you believe it would be best for your family or for the sake of winning others to the kingdom, do it quietly, kindheartedly, and without criticism. To do otherwise only drives away those who need Christ and His church.

Lastly, had the believers in Paul's era not given back to the church the way they did, the church would not be what it is today, which is the most powerful force on earth representing God and His salvation message. Hopefully, the same will be said of your family's generation in a couple of hundred years from now; that is, unless Christ returns before then.

Teachable Moment

The heart of this chapter is to seek a relationship with a church where your family can both give and receive. Therefore, picture an evening meal together with your children. In our family, preparation for the evening meal involved the whole family, including me; no one got a free ride. When our kids were young, they usually helped set the table, cleared it afterwards, and assisted in washing and drying the dishes. When they got older, they would do some of the cooking on certain occasions. We involved them for several reasons, it shared the work load, prepared them for the future when they would be on their own, and it bonded us, which often happens when working together.

This can be compared to the kind of relationship your family should have with the church. You are the church in this illustration and your children represent your family. When preparing a meal, the church (parent) takes on most of the responsibility of the ministry, and just like your children who help you with a meal, your entire family should likewise serve in the church. If your family does this, good results will come; the church staff won't be overloaded, your family will become more equipped to do ministry, and a wonderful bond with the church will develop.

Therefore, pick a special meal every once in a while where everyone in your family helps. Then, before saying grace, teach your children this comparison so that they will always remember the importance of giving to and receiving from the church.

The following verses referenced in this chapter can be found in sequence on my web site, www.tmoments.com. Click on the Book Resources button located on the home page.

I Corinthians 9:5; Romans 16:1; Galatians 6:10; Ephesians 2:19; I Timothy 3:2,4,5; Matthew 13:53-54; Matthew 5:1-2; Luke 5:1; Matthew 5:2-9; Luke 8:24-25; Matthew 19:13-14; I Corinthians 3:1-2; Hebrews 5:12-14; II Timothy 3:16-17; John 7:18; John 12:43; II Timothy 4:2-3; Acts 2:27; John 4:9-10; Matthew 5:1-2; Matthew 23:2-4; Galatians 5:13

FIFTEEN
GREEN-HOUSING
YOUR CHILDREN

(A child's relationship with school)

"I do not ask You to take them out of the world ..."
(John 17:15)

The fourth relationship that helps prepare your children for the world and their future is their schooling. It is in this setting that your children will spend much of their time outside the home. Their schoolmates, friends, teachers, and others in their school activities will have a profound affect and influence on them.

For some, a school choice is an option, but for others it isn't; it all depends upon your particular set of circumstances. Regardless of your freedom to choose or not, the school environment your children will experience should spiritually accomplish at least two things beyond the obvious goal of providing them a good education. The first is to provide protection against the destructive influences of the world. The second, and equally as important, is to provide an opportunity for your children to be exposed to those impacted by worldly influences, so that they have the opportunity to lead the lost to the Lord. In respect to this, most of the school alternatives are analyzed below. Each has its own set of strengths and weaknesses in regard to protection from, and exposure to, worldly influences.

In pursuit of this balance between protection and exposure, the *green-housing* portion of Paul and Jesus' lives and ministries will be drawn upon. *Green-housing* is a gardening expression used when plants are removed from the outside elements to a glassed-in green house for protection.[1] Plants are still able to receive the sun's rays which are needed for survival because of the glass structure. When *green-housed* plants are strong enough, they are put back outside where they belong. In respect to Paul, God *green-housed* him right after his conversion, and Christ *green-housed* the disciples before they took on the world. In both cases, protection and exposure were necessary for them to do God's bidding. This is also the case now with your children who are God's great ambassadors to those in this century.

Paul

When Paul accepted Christ as Lord and Savior, he was very much like a new plant in need of *green-housing* in that he was young, vulnerable, and untested. His new found faith, which was quite controversial at the time, made him subject to many personal attacks. *(Acts 9:1-19)* After all, he was not just someone who had quietly searched and found a Savior, but rather, a renowned enemy of Christ and one of Satan's best instruments for destroying Christianity. God, therefore, *green-housed* Paul before Satan and others could unleash a tornado of wrath against him for making such a turnabout decision. So, not long after Paul made his faith known, he was sheltered in Arabia, Damascus, and Tarsus, areas far from the nerve centers of Jerusalem and the great cities of the Roman Empire. *(Galatians 1:15-19)* His time in God's *green house* allowed him to be protected, grow in his new relationship with Christ, and study God's Word. When his time was completed, he left his place of safety, ready to accept and fulfill his duties as a representative and disciple of Christ.

God never *green-housed* Paul again. The only time he would ever experience such a safe and controlled surrounding again was when he entered heaven. The important point of this is that *green-housing* served a great purpose in Paul's life; it protected him at a time in his life when he needed it. It was not for a long period of time, because God wanted him, as He wants all of us including our children, to be out in the world winning others for the kingdom.

Jesus

Jesus used *green-housing* in His ministry, too. He employed it early with the disciples, whom He considered His family. *(Matthew 12:46-50)* He did not ask a lot during their first year together other than follow and observe. During this protective, *green-house* time, the disciples witnessed miracles, saw Him confront the religious establishment, and heard Him preach many times before others. *(John 2:1-11, 13-17; Matthew 4:23-25)*

After the disciples' *green-housing* was over, Jesus involved them more and more in His ministry, regularly increasing their exposure to the world. At the end of the first year, He sent them out in pairs to preach the Gospel, heal the sick, raise the dead, and cast demons out of the afflicted. *(Matthew 10:5-8)* As the disciples grew in their faith, Jesus gradually withdrew His every day protection. It was not that He stopped loving them, but He knew that in order for their faith to grow, they had to experience life's fears, defeats, and worldly challenges first hand. *(John 15:20)* During these post *green-house* days, Jesus let their faith be tested several times. He could have interceded, or asked the Spirit to intervene, but He didn't for the sake of their maturity. If Jesus had not done this, the disciples would never have become effective representing Him to the world, because they would have been too afraid and inexperienced. Therefore, protective *green-housing* was vital to the disciple's spiritual development but so was exposing them to the world; no less than what you also need to do with your children as you raise them.

Parent Application

Therefore, choosing the most suitable school environment for your children is very important if you are going to protect (*green-house*) them from the world and win the world over to God at the same time. In respect to this, the following observations are organized under the headings: *Public Education, Christian Schools, Private Schools,* and *Home Schooling.*

In our family, just about every one of these school settings was experienced at one time or another, each fulfilling God's purpose for us. Both my wife and I attended, taught, or had our kids in public, Christian, and private schools, and our son and his wife home schooled their children for a season.

Public Education

The public school can be a good experience for your children depending upon the school. There are public schools that should be avoided if possible due to their lack of performance, values, and safety. When we moved to Los Angeles, the school district where our kids were to attend was not acceptable because it lacked protection and strong academics. On the other hand, the public school they attended in Colorado was a very good one, because teachers were respected, good citizenship amongst the students was prevalent, academic standards were high, and safety was assured. Whether your public school is like the one in Los Angeles, Colorado, or somewhere in between, it can be a good experience and definitely God's will for your kids to be there.

The protection (*green-housing*) and strengthening your children will need, though, may have to come from you at the end of each day, as well as from those who can help you at church. And don't forget, that no matter how challenging a public school may become at times, the questions and dilemmas your children bring home can serve as great opportunities to teach them what is right and wrong from the Scripture. It has often been said that in life we learn the most when we are challenged or put under pressure; pray that this will be the case with your children if they attend public school.

Along with what your children can learn from you during their public school years, there comes the opportunity for them to share Christ with their schoolmates and friends. If your children can do this while they are young and under your *green-house* protection, they will likely do it throughout their lives.

Further, rest assured that your children are not the only ones God has assigned to the public school. God loves the lost and wishes all to be saved, so He most likely has placed Christian teachers, administrators, coaches, and other parents there, too. *(II Peter 3:9)* Find them; they will be great resources, especially when your children need some protective *green-housing* while on campus.

There are challenges in having your kids in public school; factors you need to consider before making a decision to put them there. Many of the children with whom they attend school will not have the same Christian and biblical values yours will, and neither will the school. Some (or several) of their teachers may be deadened or opposed to Christianity, which might be reflected in their teaching and daily influence. The public school curriculum, by and large, will not support your biblical views on key issues like creation, the make up of the family, and evolution. At one time, it did. In fact the very first public schools in America were required by Congress not only to teach academics but religion (Christianity) and morality (Bible) as stated in Article III of the Northwest Ordinance of 1789.[2] Quite a change from then till now, wouldn't you say?

Regardless of the negatives that surround attendance at public school, the positives more times than not win out. This is especially true when you do some good *green-housing,* that is, not letting your children get overexposed to worldly influences on campus.

Christian Schools

Christian schools can also be another good choice for your kids. When I mention Christian schools I group both Protestant and Catholic together, even though there are certain theological differences. Christian schools have at least four very notable distinctives. First, the teachers are Christians who can help reinforce the spiritual values you are building within your children at home and at church. Secondly, the curriculums are either Bible-based or secular-based with a Christian perspective. Thirdly, the students are usually under a firmer code of discipline and the unruly can be asked to leave the school if necessary. Fourthly, kids are surrounded by other schoolmates who share similar Christian values.

There are two types of Christian schools to consider. One is open to all students whether Christian or not, and these schools are called by different names. For the sake of our discussion I'll refer to them as open Christian campuses. The other type of Christian school accepts Christians only and will be referred to as Christian-only campuses. The Christian commitment requirement varies in Christian-only campuses; some call for only the child to be a Christian, others stipulate that both child and parent must be.

The overall drawback of Christian schools is usually financial; they simply don't have the funds to do all that public schools can do. Therefore, they can't always provide the best facilities, hire the most qualified teachers, or offer all of the necessary programs to meet the needs of the gifted and special need students. Regardless of these challenges they can still offer your children a great deal, especially in respect to spirituality, character development, and safety.

Open-Christian campuses

The open Christian campus accepts both Christian and non-Christian students. It is sometimes referred to as a mission-focused school because of this. It can be a great choice, especially if you want your children to be in a learning environment where their faith can both be protected and challenged at the same time. With dedicated Christian teachers, integrated Christian curriculum, and many schoolmates who know Christ, your children's faith is set to be protected, just as Paul's was when he was *green-housed* by God. In addition to this, your children's knowledge about the world and the way it thinks can also be grasped because of the presence of non-Christian students and families at the school.

If you choose a Christian campus like this, have the expectation that both good and bad things can occur, but in the midst of this you have a well trained and dedicated staff to help your children all along the way. They will do all they can to protect your children's walk with God, aid in understanding worldly thinking and temptation, and equip them to reach the lost on campus for Christ.

Of course, a school like this can also give you many great opportunities as a parent to be an example and witness to other parents. *Abstaining from gossip, refusing to criticize your children's adult leaders in their extra-curricular activities, and not demanding that they get the best perceived teacher, demonstrate what the Christian should reflect.* It also models for your children one of the most important principles Paul wrote about in the Christian life, putting the needs of others first.

> *...but with humility of mind regard one another as more important than yourselves; do not merely look out for your own personal interests, but also for the interests of others. Have this attitude in yourselves which was also in Christ Jesus. (Philippians 2: 3-5)*

There are a few drawbacks to an open Christian campus. If, for instance, the school neglects its mission to bring non-Christian students and families to Christ, then it risks losing control of the campus to them. This happens when school leadership doesn't have a clear plan or desire to fulfill this mission. It also occurs when non-Christian students outnumber Christians. The negative outcome varies depending upon the campus. In my experience, I have seen the worst case scenario where the overall student character on campus was hardly recognizable as Christian. I have seen students do one, or several of the following: cheat in the classroom, haze or maliciously gossip about others, drink alcohol, do drugs, have sex, and display terrible sportsmanship during athletic competitions. Unfortunately, the parents of these kids generally didn't care as they were the same in character themselves.

If your children ever attend a Christian school where this becomes the situation, that is, where worldly thinking and behavior is winning out, I suggest you make a school change. If you stay, keep a close watch over your children and join together with other like-minded parents to try and turn things around.

Christian-only campuses

The second of the Christian school alternatives is a school for Christians only. These are sometimes called discipleship schools because they focus on equipping believers, not reaching out to non-Christians. In these schools, students are required to profess Christ as Savior before entering. If they are too young to do so, the testimony of one or both parents usually suffices. In some cases, both student and parents must be Christians, and in a few schools church membership required. How an entering student or family demonstrates their Christian testimony varies from school to school. When I was a superintendent of a Christian school like this, my school board determined that I interview each family before issuing an acceptance. This was not a tedious task for me by any means. In fact, I looked forward each spring to listening to dozens of new faith stories, each unique in their own way.

My most memorable interview was with a father and mother who thought they were Christians, but weren't. In fact, each was a member of a different cult that was parading as a Christian church. As I shared the way to Christ with them, each became immediately smitten and desirous to receive Him as Lord and Savior. Thus right then and there, in my office on a beautiful afternoon, they prayed to receive Christ. Afterward, an immediate peace came over them that only the Spirit could have brought. Time proved their commitment was real, for both began attending our church and sought to be discipled by other Christians. In the years to come, they became dedicated members.

There are some wonderful positives to a Christian-only campus. Like open Christian schools, teachers are dedicated to the Lord, but in the classroom, there can be even greater freedom to teach the Christian point of view on every issue, including errors and inaccuracies seen in other non-Christian religions. Sometimes on an open Campus, these errors and inaccuracies are avoided because students of these non-Christian religions might be offended or driven even further away from Christianity. I know this to be true because I worked as both a teacher and an administrator in an open Christian campus. It was not as though we were compromising what we believed, but the goal was to win over non-Christian students to Christ; criticizing their beliefs was determined not to be the path to accomplish this. However, with a Christian-only campus, this is not an issue and the whole truth about whatever or whoever is in error can be discussed and taught.

Another positive in a Christian-only campus is complete liberty for students to openly express their faith without fear of rejection. The absence of non-Christians and their opposition makes this possible.

Classroom sizes are also a positive; for the most part, they are smaller because of the entrance restrictions. This can be a real advantage for your children. As a superintendent where class sizes were small, sometimes no more that fifteen to a classroom, students received much more individualized attention from teachers. This can benefit your child and should be considered. In my experience, there wasn't a child who didn't do better in a smaller classroom, especially those who were a little behind or who came from broken families where support at home was not always provided.

Like other school alternatives, there are also some drawbacks to consider in regard to a Christian-only campus. In many cases, because of the Christian-only stipulation, there was smaller enrollment. This was a plus for classroom size but ended up as a negative when it came to school budget revenue. Less money for a school usually meant inadequate to fair facilities, outdated curriculum, struggling sports and music programs, and mediocre libraries and computer labs.

Another great drawback is the lack of exposure to non-Christians, those who need a Christian's friendship, influence, and testimony. Even though such exposure might bring your children into contact with wrong behavior or worldly influence, they need to be around this imperfect influence so they can learn how to deal with it and minister to those under its influence.

The last drawback is what attendance at a Christian-only school might do to your children's experience at church. If they are taught the Bible all week by professional Christian teachers, they may end up too waterlogged with biblical principles to be interested in what a volunteer Sunday school teacher may teach. With all of the teaching received at school, your children may benefit more from a situation where they can apply what they have learned. Direct application is generally not the focus of most churches on Sunday mornings as they usually center on teaching those who have been in a non-Christian environment all week. Accordingly, if your children are in a Christian school during the week, don't be surprised if they become lax or even bored with church on Sunday; they need a balance of receiving and giving, the kind of balance Jesus gave His disciples.

Sad to say, when I was a youth pastor, the high school kids in my group who attended Christian-only schools were often the least vibrant and involved. They knew the Scripture but couldn't put it to good use in their own lives. They often caused most of the problems at my Bible studies, youth activities, and camps, and they seldom, if ever, shared their faith with others. This wasn't due to not being taught well at school, but because they had no immediate involvement in the world to test what they had learned. Subsequently, as good as a Christian-only school can be, it has the potential to over *green-house* your children unless you provide a situation where they can be exposed to non-Christians and worldly thinking.

Private Schools

Private schools can be a good option; they are often funded well and generally not officially linked to any religious organization. Their rules and regulations are typically firm, not allowing the kind of negative behavior that sometimes plagues public schools. Many have nice facilities with computer labs, music rooms, cafeteria, libraries, gym, and athletic fields. In respect to your faith, most are open to letting your children express it as long as it doesn't cause an uproar with other's beliefs.

There are challenges to the private school as well, such as the expense of attending. Private schools can vary significantly in this, some as costly as a pricy college or university. You also need to realize that although your children may be in a better learning and behavioral environment than a public school, private schools may be very much aligned with the public school in respect to God. Some teachers might be Christian, but they could also be agnostic or atheist. When it comes to the Bible, the private school would most likely teach it as a piece of literature or even as a book of myths, depending upon the teacher.

Another possible challenge to a private school is unfairness. Sometimes the wealthy in the school get their own way, even if it means evading or bending the rules. Private schools charge a lot for tuition, but this is not enough to pay all of the bills. Consequently, the wealthy are tapped for donations, which can bring with it a demand for preferential treatment. In most situations, these parents get it, possibly at the expense of one of your children.

Home Schooling

Although home schooling is the last alternative discussed, it doesn't mean it is the least of the choices. On the contrary, it can be a very good school situation for your kids, depending upon at least three things: your ability to teach, your children's response to learning academics from you, and your plan to involve them with other children, both Christian and non-Christian.

The positives to home schooling are personalized instruction, safety, the option to choose the curriculum, direct control over discipline, an opportunity to develop a Christian world view in all subjects, separation from the negative influences in a typical school, and the flexibility to do as many field trips as you want in response to what your children are learning.

There are challenges in home schooling which also must be considered, especially in respect to protectively over *green-housing* your children. Since they are with you all day and everyday for their schooling, it is likely they will not get to know others their age as they should, and in particular those who need to know the Lord. Without such interaction your children may not be equipped to build the necessary social skills to win over others for Christ. In fact, fear, misunderstanding, shyness, or lack of confidence with others can result when children are overly *green-housed*, as can happen in home schooling. As a result, you must do something in the schooling experience to counter this if you truly want them to become God's representatives and ambassadors to this world.

In my experience as a teacher, I had some wonderful home-schooled students transfer into my classes from time to time. Many came in advanced in their class work and were quite pleasant and cooperative. My greatest struggle with them, however, was that some came in with varying degrees of diminished skills relating to others. On average, it took me about half the school year to get them where they needed to be in this respect.

Other challenges in home schooling include getting assignments done well and on time. In home schooling, if an assignment isn't done well, then it can be redone without penalty. If not turned in on time, that date can be changed or extended. Who is there to demand or require differently? This is not the way it's done in higher education or in the work place. College assignments must be done well and turned in on time. If not then most professors will give a failing grade. Most employers will let workers go, (this includes your kids when they get older) if they don't do what they should, when they should.

If all of these potential drawbacks are dealt with, then home schooling can be a very good way to go, especially if you live in a community where public schools are suspect and Christian campuses are weak or unaffordable.

My final caution is that I wouldn't home school for more than a season in your children's lives. Just as Jesus *green-housed* His disciples for a short time, perhaps you should do likewise with your kids. You don't want them to fall prey to the world, but as the Scripture says, you don't want to isolate them from the world, either.

"I do not ask You to take them out of the world, but to keep them from the evil one. They are not of the world, even as I am not of the world. As You sent Me into the world, I also have sent them into the world." (John 17:15-16, 18)

Final Thoughts

Finally, don't feel bad if you move your children from one school situation to another. Their needs, as well as your circumstances, may change from time to time. They are not going to be any less prepared for the future whether they attend one, two, or many schools during their life time. It doesn't matter the type of school, as long as you know and work with the advantages and disadvantages of each. As I stated, my children went to several different schools while growing up, both public and Christian. They adjusted to each, as your kids will if you keep trusting God to help you balance protecting them from the world, while reaching out to others at the same time.

Teachable Moment

Every morning when taking a devotional walk, a school crossing guard usually helps me cross one of the busier streets on my trek. The street is near a school, so it stands to reason he is there to help. Of course his primary job is to assist school children, but he is very kind to help me, also.

Such can be a Teachable Moment reminder of the necessity to protectively *green- house* your children from the negative influences of the world during their school years, while at the same time exposing them to it for the sake of winning those under its control. The crossing guard in this illustration is you. If you have ever watched a crossing guard work, he or she does a lot to ensure children's safety when they cross a busy street. He raises his stop sign, steps into the street, and then escorts the children to the other side. In a way this is what you do with your children when you teach them God's Word, monitor their friends, be a good example, and help choose the right school environment for them.

Like the cars that stop and take notice when the crossing guard walks into the middle of the street, so the world will also stop, put on its brakes, and take notice of how you walk your children through the difficult and sometimes dangerous problems and challenges of this life.

Thus the next time you see a crossing guard leading kids across a busy street, think of this illustration. When your kids are old enough, take them to a crossing guard location and have them add their own thoughts and parallels. Remember, they will be parents one day and play the same role you are playing with them right now.

The following verses referenced in this chapter can be found in sequence on my web site, www.tmoments.com. Click on the Book Resources button located on the home page.

Acts 9:1-19; Galatians 1:15-19; Matthew 12:46-50; John 2:1-11; John 2:13-17; Matthew 4:23-25; Matthew 10:5-8; John 15: 20; II Peter 3:9

SIXTEEN

CAMP ASSURANCE

(A family's relationship to a fallen world)

You are from God, little children, and have overcome them; because greater is
He who is in you than he who is in the world.
(I John 4:4)

As advanced as the 21st century is in so many ways, it still creates great hardship for most parents trying to raise children in an atmosphere of morality and godliness. Amidst the progress made in areas like education, technology, medicine, and food production, we are still overflowing with unparalleled hatred, greed, sexual grossness, drug and alcohol addiction, man-worship, prejudice, and occult practices. Sadly, this is but a short list of sins and wrong doings. *(Galatians 5:19-21)* Therefore a fifth important relationship to prepare your children for the future is with the world and the author of so much of its evil, Satan.

Before moving to the discussion of how to relate to a world dominated by sin and Satan, I want to share with you a personal story where I saw his ugly impact, but I also witnessed the incredible forward thinking and powerful response of God. The story is unforgettable, enough to serve as a Teachable Moment for your kids one day.

Camp Assurance

As mentioned in Chapter 4, I received my first official, full-time ministry position in 1971. I was hired as a youth pastor for a church in Seattle, Washington, and married my fiancé, Myrna, soon after. Both my wife and I were very excited to begin our lives doing youth ministry together. We had both grown up in Southern California, so the move to Washington was new for both of us. It suited us well, though, because we both wanted to see life in other parts of the country, especially the beautiful Northwest. As the new youth pastor, I had many hopes, dreams, and expectations as many do when they first enter ministry. All I could see during that first year were the positives ahead in serving one of God's churches.

Over the rest of my 40 years of ministry, I learned the other side, too, which included debates and fights over doctrine, music, worship, preaching style, evangelism, and of course, battles between pastors, church members, and leaders. However, for this brief time, God protected me from all of that by first giving me a wonderful older pastor under which to serve.

Reverend Brown was a pastor in his late 50s when I met him, as old as I am now. From the outset, he was very kind, encouraging, and protective. Knowing what was ahead, he took me under his wing right away, spending time getting to know me and making my first months as smooth as possible. Years later, I learned that he defended me on many occasions with different church members. Some didn't particularly like the young people at our church, but Reverend Brown did and told me so many times.

In addition to memorable remarks, I will never forget the support he gave me during one of the biggest tests of my ministry. It was a situation that occurred at Camp Assurance, a spring weekend retreat. College and high school age students attended one weekend, and junior high the next. The college and high school camp went great; there were no problems as lives were impacted, God was honored, and young people came home strengthened in their faith. The second Camp Assurance with the junior high though, was a bit different, because the junior high students in my youth group were challenging.

Camp Assurance was located in Central Washington at a beautiful campground, but just off the property was a concrete canal filled with rushing water. The canal had a very strong current and was dangerous. There were ropes stretched across it about every two hundred yards so that if anyone slipped in, they could get out by grabbing one. As I learned later, those ropes were useless life-saving devices, because over time, they had grown too slippery to grasp. There were *"Keep Away"* warning signs all along the canal.

During the first night at the junior high camp, I explained the danger of the canal to the junior high kids, and I assured them we would send any of them home if they got near the canal. I was very emphatic, especially with some of the more challenging boys. After the singing, skits, and message was over that first night, everyone headed for their rooms with their counselors. During their devotional time, one more review of the rules was given by their counselors about the canal restrictions. As I walked by each room, everything seemed in control and surprisingly quiet. I was relieved; I thought that maybe the concerns about this group were a bit exaggerated.

Early the next morning, screams rang out at a distance from the cabin. I was already up working on a message for that evening, so I was the first to hear these cries for help. In anguish, I ran quickly toward the cries as they turned into louder and louder yells. As I ran, I realized I was sprinting in the direction of the canal. It took me only a few minutes to get there, and when I did, I saw one boy crying along the canal bank and another soaking wet from just getting out. A third boy who had been with them was nowhere to be seen. Bobby, John, and Mike obviously had not heeded the warnings given in our meeting, and even turned a deaf ear to their counselor, who happened to be an elder at our church.

As I questioned Bobby and John sitting on the bank, a few other counselors arrived to help. Bobby and John continued to explain that they snuck out and were merely throwing rocks and pine cones at a dead deer carcass in the canal, until Mike slipped and fell in. John immediately jumped in to help, but quickly got out when the water's current began taking him down stream. Bobby stayed on shore to help John. They both saw Mike grab for one of the ropes stretching across the canal, but he couldn't hold on. As he vanished down stream, Bobby and John began to yell for help until I showed up.

While listening to the boys' accounts with growing anxiety, I immediately sent the counselors and the two boys back to camp to call for Mountain Rescue. As they took off, two other counselors arrived and joined me as I began to run down the side of the canal to catch up with Mike. I felt it would not take long before we caught him; I was a pretty fast runner and so were the two counselors with me.

After running about two miles, we came to a split in the canal where one went to the right and the other to the left. We followed the split to the right first, which eventually disappeared into a large funnel, like one you might go down at a water park. No Mike to be seen, though, at the end of our effort. We knelt down, caught our breath, and then ran back to the split, where we continued down the other part of the canal. We ran another four miles or so before it also disappeared into a huge funnel. Still no Mike! By then, we were perplexed and exhausted.

About that time one of the Mountain Rescue teams showed up in a helicopter. When we explained our run down the canal, the leader of the team told us that each of those funnels went underground and reappeared in a large river just beyond our view. He told us he would circle back to see if Mike had gotten out of the canal on his own. We continued to walk another mile down toward the river below, but found no trace of Mike.

With more units of Mountain Rescue showing up, we headed back to camp, retracing our steps along the way. We frequently yelled out his name, hoping he would hear us. Deep down, I believe each of us thought Mike would be there when we got back with an incredible story to tell. When we arrived back at camp, more squads of the Mountain Rescuers were there using our camp as a staging area. Helicopters were coming and going and my heart sank!

Of course, now I had to inform the church, call the parents, and all the while keep the camp going. Needless to say, I was a bit overwhelmed until Reverend Brown stepped in to help shoulder some of the burden. He got the prayer chain going at church, instructed an elder at the camp not to leave my side, and went over and met with the parents.

Later, as helicopters flew back and forth, I decided to gather the counselors to pray for Mike, as well as his family who were on their way up to camp. Even at this juncture, we held hope for Mike's return. A couple hours after our prayers, Mike's parents arrived. They were distraught, as you can imagine, but amazingly ready to accept the outcome whatever it might be. Reverend Brown had apparently counseled them well and did not hesitate to tell them what was hoped and prayed for, but also what could be. Don, the elder mentioned earlier, was actually the first on the scene to meet them as they arrived. When I saw them, I rushed over to express my sorrow and regret as best I could. I told them the entire camp had been praying for them and Mike all day, and that the Mountain Rescue teams were doing all they could to locate Mike.

As the afternoon passed into the evening, the search was officially called off. There was no Mike to be found anywhere. The Mountain Rescue team said they would continue the search in the morning and encouraged the parents to return home. Reluctantly, with great disappointment and distress, Mike's parents tearfully made their way back to Seattle.

That evening after dinner, our entire group gathered together for a time of prayer and teaching. Mike and his family were at the center of our prayers, but God and His love for Mike was the theme of my teaching. I can't remember all that I said, but when I was finished, just about every young person in that room either received Christ for the first time or committed their lives to follow Him thereafter.

In the morning, the rescue attempts resumed, but Mike could not be found. As our group readied itself to leave camp for home, it was quite unsettling to leave him behind. On the way back many of us continued to pray for Mike, and others made it a point to console his parents when they returned.

Three weeks passed before we heard from the Mountain Rescue team again; they called to say they had found Mike's body. It had been found by some campers who saw it washed up on shore some 20 miles from the camp. The rescue team surmised that Mike most likely had drowned after going through one of the funnels.

Reverend Brown's message at Mike's funeral was comforting and true to Scripture. He talked about a number of things: God's love for Mike, the world which can draw any of us to disaster, and the Lord's responsibility and control over all events no matter how disastrous or difficult. We all listened intently, for if Mike could be taken, so could any of us.

Over the next few years, most in our youth group accomplished many great things for God. One of the key reasons for this I believe was the tragedy, for it got them thinking about God and their own mortality. After returning from that weekend, they read their Bibles, prayed often, served others, lived reputable lives at school, and even won many of their friends to the Lord. Even today, many still minister with the same zeal they did over 40 years ago.

What's Ahead?

What happened to Mike was tragic, but more tragic was what led him to the canal bank that day. Like all of us, he was born into this world with a sin nature, that if not dealt with, can easily be influenced by Satan and his many worldly urgings and influences. *(Romans 5:12, 18; I Timothy 3:7)* With Mike, these particular urgings swayed him to disregard danger, refuse counsel, and do just what he wanted to do. I personally don't know if Mike was a Christian, perhaps he was, and this decision of his was just a mere lapse of faith. But I do know by experience and God's Word, Satan and his worldly influences must be fought against, otherwise similar fates can happen, even to your children.

The next two chapters of this section, *Combating Satan's Influences* and *Equipping Your Children to Win Others for Christ,* focus on preparing your children for the world they are in now and the one they must face in the future. Both will strengthen your children, as well as help prevent tragedies similar to what happened to Mike. Tragedies that may not include drowning in a raging canal, but rather drowning in a sea of rebellion, drugs, love of self, alcohol, greed, love of power, sex, love of security, and unbelief.

Final Thoughts

In respect to Reverend Brown, I continued to serve as his youth minister until I left for seminary a few years later. No matter where the Lord took me, we always stayed in close contact until he died. Before the Lord took Reverend Brown, I had the opportunity to see him one last time. I flew up to Seattle after I heard he had a severe heart attack, and probably wouldn't survive. When I got to the hospital, there were strict orders that no one except a family member be allowed to see him, but I snuck through the back corridors of the hospital anyway until I found his room. Upon entering, I found him sitting up in bed and surprisingly alert. As I started to apologize for breaking the rules, he quickly interrupted and said, "Kent! I am so glad to see you. You know you are like a son to me; you warm my heart being here." We talked for several minutes and then prayed together. When I left, I felt he had ministered to me more than I had ministered to him, but that was always the way with Reverend Brown, you could never out-encourage him. He will be one of the first I want to see when I get to heaven; one of the first!

The following verses referenced in this chapter can be found in sequence on my web site, www.tmoments.com. Click on the Book Resources button located on the home page.

Galatians 5:19-21; Romans 5:12, 18; I Timothy 3:7

SEVENTEEN
BANGING ON THEIR GATES, TOO!

(Combating Satan's influences)

Be of sober spirit, be on the alert, your adversary, the devil, prowls around like a roaring lion, seeking someone to devour.
(I Peter 5:8)

Lucifer, Satan, and the Devil are just a few of the names ascribed to an exceedingly wicked demonic being mentioned throughout the Bible. *(Isaiah 14:12; Mark 1:13; Matthew 13:19; Luke 4:3)* He is not merely a symbol of evil but as real as you and I are today. For the sake of simplicity, I will refer to him as Satan throughout this chapter.

Historically, Satan was once a great angel, created and loved by God. He was cast out of heaven when his sinful pride conquered his heart. It was not enough for Satan to be one of God's greatest creations, he wanted more, to be God himself. *(Isaiah 14:12-17)* But he couldn't, and this drove him to be God's opposite: a rebellious, violent, profane, self-seeking, hateful, and unloving living being.

You {Satan} were in Eden, the garden of God; every precious stone was your covering: The ruby, the topaz and the diamond; the beryl, the onyx and the jasper; the lapis lazuli, the turquoise and the emerald; and the gold, the workmanship of your settings and sockets, were in you. On the day that you were created they were prepared. You were the anointed cherub who covers, and I placed you there. You were on the holy mountain of God; You walked in the midst of the stones of fire. You were blameless in your ways from the day you were created. Until unrighteousness was found in you. By the abundance of your trade you were internally filled with violence, and you sinned; therefore I have cast you as profane from the mountain of God. And I have destroyed you, oh covering cherub, from the midst of the stones of fire. Your heart was lifted up because of your beauty; you corrupted your wisdom by reason of your splendor. I cast you to the ground; I put you before kings, that they may see you. (Ezekiel 28:13-17)

To make your children aware of Satan is very important, because he is still alive and well today with vast access to their world. Like other generations before, your children may also experience his terrible influence, overwhelming power, and exceeding wickedness. Without a plan, a good one based on the Scripture, your children may fall prey to various influences and temptations as others have before.

To understand Satan's impact on those in this world, including believers, Paul's insight into two of his main strategies, legalism and immorality, will be studied. In addition to this, how Jesus battled Satan while on earth will be reviewed, particularly how He put up a good offense and defense against him.

Paul

In Paul's writings, Satan was presented as one of the most destructive, evil, and scheming beings ever created.

> *Finally, be strong in the Lord and in the strength of His might. Put on the full armor of God, so that you will be able to stand firm against the schemes of the devil. For our struggle is not against flesh and blood, but against the rulers, against the powers, against the world forces of this darkness, against the spiritual forces of wickedness in the heavenly places. (Ephesians 6:10-12)*

Paul identified several modes of Satan's attacks; two of the most prominent were legalism (self-made, religious 'dos' and 'don'ts') and immorality (no right or wrongs). Legalism was usually directed toward the church and immorality toward a rebellious and unbelieving world.

Legalism

The key characteristic of legalism was dependence on visible good works for salvation and daily living rather than dependence on God through faith. Satan's ploy was simple; get Christians to focus exclusively on themselves, particularly in respect to how they appeared to God and others. Both Paul and John wrote of this legalistic approach to God in the following passages.

> *For by grace you have been saved through faith; and that not of yourselves, it is the gift of God; not as a result of works, so that no one may boast. (Ephesians 2:8-9)*

If you have died with Christ to the elementary principles of the world, why, as if you were living in the world, do you submit yourself to decrees, such as, "Do not handle, do not taste, do not touch." These are matters which have, to be sure, the appearance of wisdom in self-made religion and self-abasement and severe treatment of the body, but are of no value against fleshly indulgence. (Colossians 2:20-23)

Therefore they said to Him, "What shall we do, so that we may work the works of God?" Jesus answered and said to them, "This is the work of God that you believe in Him whom He has sent." (John 6: 28-29)

Legalism came to the church in different ways, usually beginning with false teachers who were bound up in self-glory, not God's glory. *(II Corinthians 11:13-15)* They taught those who would listen to put their confidence in them as leaders, as well as in the various rules, interpretations, customs, and traditions they espoused. What the Scripture actually taught about grace, forgiveness, and freedom in Christ was only important if it agreed with the views and applications of these legalistic leaders. *(I Timothy 1:3-7)* The impact of legalism hurt several churches in Paul's day as it hurts churches in our day, which was Satan's purpose. Many left the church and turned away from the Lord because of it. Your children might do the same after they have grown up if legalism dominates the church you attend.

I am amazed that you are so quickly deserting Him who called you by the grace of Christ, for a different gospel; which is really not another; only there are some who are disturbing you and want to distort the gospel of Christ. (Galatians 1:6)

Immorality

In addition to trying to destroy the church through legalism, Satan also went after unbelievers in the world through its opposite, immorality. Now, this is not to say that Satan did not also use immorality to destroy those in the church, too; he did, whenever possible.

Paul describes immorality and all of its adjoining sins in several of his letters to the churches. Here are just of few of those descriptions written to the churches at Corinth, Colossae, and Ephesus.

I wrote you in my letter not to associate with immoral people; I did not at all mean with the immoral people of this world, or with the covetous and swindlers, or with idolaters, for then you would have to go out of the world. But actually, I wrote to you not to associate with any so-called brother if he is an immoral person, or covetous, or an idolater, or a reviler, or a drunkard, or a swindler—not even to eat with such a one. (I Corinthians 5:9-11)

Therefore consider the members of your earthly body as dead to immorality, impurity, passion, evil desire, and greed, which amount to idolatry. (Colossians 3:5)

Now the deeds of the flesh are evident, which are: immorality, impurity, sensuality, idolatry, sorcery, enmities, strife, jealousy, outbursts of anger, disputes, dissensions, factions, envying, drunkenness, carousing, and things like these... (Ephesians 5:19-21)

To deal with Satan's immoral influences on the world, Paul successfully combated it with faith, and his knowledge of when to stand against or flee from it. Illustratively, Paul was like a great football team with an excellent offense and defense. *(II Timothy 4:1-3; Acts 26:21-28)* When on offense, he attacked the world with the Gospel, preaching Christ in some of the most immoral places on earth. When on defense, he knew when to stand his ground or flee according to the situation. This is a tactic your family needs to apply when defending against the influences and temptations of this world. Prayer, seeking direction in the Word, and getting advice from other believers can help you know when to stand firm or flee.

Stand firm therefore, having girded your loins with truth, and having put on the breastplate of righteousness. (Ephesians 6:14)

Flee immorality every other sin that a man commits is outside the body, but the immoral man sins against his own body. (I Corinthians 6:18)

Jesus

Jesus fought countless battles and counter battles against Satan. Jesus being the Son of God didn't scare Satan off; he went after Jesus the minute He arrived on earth in Bethlehem. Through King Herod, troops were sent to slay Jesus at His birth. In the attempt, all of the male children in

Bethlehem two years and under were slain to make sure Jesus was killed. The effort failed because the Father and Spirit steered Joseph and Mary to Egypt before the terrible calamity took place. *(Matthew 2:13-16)* As to the children who died that day, be assured God took every one to heaven. Unlike Satan, God's character has always reflected the desire to save mankind, not destroy it. He would not have sacrificed His own Son on the cross if this had not been so.

So it is not the will of your Father who is in heaven that one of these little ones perish. (Matthew 18:14)

Satan also attacked Jesus again right before He began His public ministry. It was in the desert after Jesus had spent 40 days praying and fasting. In this battle, Satan threw three temptations at Jesus. He first tried to influence Him to break His fast and take care of His own physical needs. The second focused on tempting Jesus to gain approval with the religious community by miraculously surviving a dive off the Temple. The third centered on Jesus attaining glory and riches with the price tag of worshiping Satan. *(Matthew 4:1-11)* Jesus repelled all three temptations, not by the means of His own divine power, but through the quotation of Scripture, a weapon he purposefully left for all believers to use, even your family, when facing the temptations of this world.

Satan's failure to win over Jesus still didn't discourage him from attacking again and again; his scheming plots acted out through Peter, Judas, and the religious leaders during His trials and crucifixion were proof of this. *(Luke 22:31; Luke 22:3)* And who knows how many other times Satan went after Jesus; John in his writings mentioned it would have taken volumes to record everything Jesus experienced while on earth. *(John 21:25)*

In fending off Satan, Jesus not only fought him one-on-one in the desert, but He also fought against the many sent against Him under Satan's influence, as was the case at the crucifixion. But Jesus didn't spend all of His time defending against Satan's various attacks; He spent it helping others and preaching the truth to them. *(Matthew 5:1-6; Matthew 8:1-3; Luke 8:27-32)* Because He did, many in Satan's camp were won over, rescued, and saved.

In the process of Jesus equipping the disciples, He delivered an incredible sermon not many days before His last trek to Jerusalem. In this message, delivered at Capernaum, Jesus began by asking the disciples who others thought He was. A few answers trickled forth, until Jesus asked emphatically, "But who do you say that I am?" Peter finally stepped forth and exclaimed, *"You are the Christ, the Son of the living God!" (Matthew 16:13-16)* Immediately Jesus responded with a very important five point lesson, which included wrestling control of the world from Satan.

Point 1   God's role in revealing truth

And Jesus said to him, "Blessed are you, Simon Barjona, because flesh and blood did not reveal this to you, but My Father who is in   heaven." (Matthew 16:17)

Point 2   Peter's role in building the church

"I also say to you that you are Peter, and upon this rock I will build My Church." (Matthew 16:18a)

Point 3   Assured victory for the church

"And the gates of Hades will not overpower it." (Matthew 16:18b)

Point 4   God's provision to build the church

"I will give you the keys of the kingdom of heaven." (Matthew 16:19a)

Point 5   Lasting value for doing God's bidding

"And whatever you bind on earth shall have been bound in heaven, and whatever you loose on earth shall have been loosed in heaven." (Matthew 16:19b)

The third point, *"the gates of Hades will not overpower it,"* often gets lost because the other four are seemingly more remembered. However if you had the background of the disciples in this setting, this wouldn't be so. In respect to the *gates,* cities during that era were protected by high walls and one or two central gates. When an enemy approached, all hurried in, shut the gates, and hoped for the best. The weakest part of a city's defense was the *gate*; if it was knocked down, the city was lost. In using this term, Jesus was telling the disciples that they were not just to defend the Gospel in a safe place that was gated from Satan's worldly influences, but they were to take the Gospel to the gates of Satan's strongholds and do battle there. If they did, then Satan and his influence on the world would eventually crumble, which is what He meant when He said, "*The gates of Hades will not prevail against it*" (the church). This is exactly what the disciples did when they later preached His Word and established churches in Rome, Corinth, Ephesus, and so many other places throughout the world.

This is something to keep in mind as you raise and disciple your children, for God doesn't just want your home to be a well-gated fortress against the world. Like the disciples He wants your family out there winning others into the kingdom, banging on their gates so to speak.

Parent Application

To prepare your children for the world influenced by Satan and his various evil influences and temptations, here are some applications to consider: *Don't Be Afraid, Build Strong Habits, Fight against Legalism and Immorality, Realize that Satan Is No Match for God, Let God Take Control,* and *Use the Sword*

Don't Be Afraid

Although Satan and his influences on this world aren't nearly as powerful as God, he cannot be taken lightly or ignored. If allowed, he will intimidate your entire family as often as possible. He won't leave your family alone even if you minimize your walk with the Lord; He just doesn't work that way. As Peter said, "*Satan is like a roaring lion*," always on the prowl to destroy one's faith, this includes your family's faith. In view of this, ***if you want your children to survive Satan's worldly influences, plan to do battle, either at his gates or yours.*** Remember, Satan didn't hesitate to go after Jesus, and he won't hesitate with your family, either. Begin by teaching your children not to be afraid, because stronger is God in you and them than Satan and all of his combined forces are in the world. If you put your trust in Him and do as the Scripture teaches, you will do just fine.

You are from God, little children, and have overcome them; because greater is He who is in you than he who is in the world. (I John 4:4)

In the story of Mike's drowning, I mentioned that many in my youth group went back home renewed in spirit to serve the Lord as never before. If Satan's ploy was to use that tragedy to keep them afraid and on the defensive about their faith, it had the opposite impact. In fact, it motivated them to play mostly on the offensive side of the ball as Jesus encouraged His disciples to do. As I look back, these kids did so many different things to bring others to Christ, that it is hard to remember all they did. Although there is one event that does stand out, one that they all did together which not only affected our church but the little community of West Seattle where we lived. The local newspaper wrote about their event as a human interest story. What they did was create, sing, and perform in a dramatic-musical play called *The Rapture* which centered on the return of Christ in the last days. Now a play, even a good one, is nothing out of the ordinary, but the enthusiastic way these kids got people to attend was, as our large sanctuary was filled the evening of *The Rapture* play. And it was filled not just with church people but with those who had never darkened the door of a church.

I was amazed when I looked out to see all who had come When we were finished with the last scene where Christians were taken up to be with Christ, several in the audience sat there contemplating what they had just seen, others responded with delight, and even some made commitments to Christ afterward. It is incredible what you can do, and become, when you don't let Satan and his influence make you afraid to display your faith and reach out to others, instead. Let this be true of you and your children, too!

Build Strong Habits

Satan's worldly influences will often hit your family at vulnerable times, as he did with Jesus at His birth and crucifixion. Such times often occur when circumstances get beyond your control, such as a loss of a job, break in a relationship, unwarranted criticism, a surprise bill, sickness, or an accident. Mike's drowning caught me and my entire youth group off guard, to say the least. At first, we didn't know what to do, but then began talking, praying, and using God's Word to gain understanding and resolve. His family did somewhat the same in their own way. Your family may never be afflicted as we were, but responding similarly can greatly help each one of you arrive at a victory when struck by Satan's influence and temptations. Accordingly, continue to build strong habits by talking things out, praying, and studying His Word together. Such will prepare you for the battles ahead; and they will come, count on it.

Fight against Legalism and Immorality

Satan is balanced in his attacks as Paul indicated. He uses both the destructive tactics of legalism and immorality to destroy a family's relationship with God. The church in which I grew up had its brand of legalism, along with the good it tried to do for the kingdom. Its list of 'dos' and 'don'ts' included: 'do' wear a shirt and tie on Sundays; 'don't' go to movies or dances, 'don't' play cards or hang out with non-Christians. It also pushed receiving Jesus as Savior over and over again every Sunday; just to make sure you didn't lose your salvation. None of these supposed acts of holiness were particularly right or wrong, but sad to say, they replaced the joy of living according to God's grace, mercy, and unconditional love.

Now the Lord is the Spirit, and where the Spirit of the Lord is, there is liberty. (II Corinthians 3:17)

In my experience as a pastor and school administrator, children raised in too much legalism often grow up rigid, self-absorbed, gossipy, judgmental, rule-dependent, competitive with other Christians, and cold toward the lost. Don't ever let this happen to your children's walk with God, for if you do then your family's relationship to the world will likely be very little. Without that relationship, the lost will remain lost; at least those in your area of influence.

Although Satan's infusion of immorality mostly impacts those in the world, it can also have a deep influence on the Christian family, as well. Unlike some past cultures where immoral practices were somewhat suppressed, covered up, or only secretly pursued, this culture today openly displays all of its shameful deeds. It does so at movie theatres, on television, in raunchy literature, on the internet, and even at school, which was once a safe and wholesome place for kids to be.

How should immorality thus be battled in your home? What kind of mindset can you give your children so they will be shielded from a culture enthralled and captured by immorality? First, make sure you monitor what your children see, what they are taught in school, and who their friends are becoming. When they see or experience something immoral, don't just restrict or shield them from it, explain why it's wrong and what its impact can be.

Most importantly, in regards to their friends, realize that the ones they choose can heavily influence them toward the good or bad, especially as they get older. The best way to handle this is to help them choose friends with good character at first, and then see how they do with others who need better character. Remember, as much as your children need good influences around them, they also need to learn how to be a good influence on others for the sake of the spread of the kingdom.

Last of all, in respect to friends, your children may differ from one another when it comes to mixing with those in need of Christ or lacking in good character. One child may do well with such a challenge; in fact, such a relationship will help build a stronger faith and reliance on God. On the other hand, another may not do so well with a friend who lives according to worldly values. Don't make a hard and rigid rule for both children, let one have friends who need to be reached, and limit that contact with the other; at least for awhile until they are ready. Isn't this what God does with each of us?

Realize that Satan Is No Match for God

While teaching your children how to battle Satan and all of his worldly forces and influences, realize that as powerful and calculating as he is, he is no match for God. *(II Peter 2:4-9)* Satan, for instance, is not omnipresent like God who can be everywhere at once. Neither is he omniscient; he doesn't know everything God does. If Satan did know all, perhaps he wouldn't have rebelled in the first place or have done the evil things he has done. Finally, Satan is also not omnipotent, for only God is all-powerful. Therefore, Satan is no match for your children, who have within them the all-present, all-knowing, and all-powerful God. All they need do when Satan strikes is to immediately put their reliance and defense on the Lord, who has promised never to leave nor forsake them. *(Romans 8:31, 38-39; John 10:27-28)*

Also be assured that when Satan attacks, it won't be in a one-on-one confrontation, for he can only be in one place at a time. In fact there are very few instances in Scripture where anyone went one-on-one with Satan, perhaps only Adam, Eve, Job, Peter, and Jesus. *(Genesis 3:1-6; Job 1:9,12; Luke 22:31; Matthew 4:3)* The Satan your children will face will be the men, women, and other children of this world who are influenced by his legalism and immorality.

Lastly, though you or your children may never face Satan one-on-one, it is okay when tempted or afflicted to refer to him as the one doing it. Many of the New Testament writers did when being attacked by his influence and forces; you can, too. *(Acts 5:3; I Corinthians 7:5)*

Let God Take Control

If you feel like one of Satan's worldly schemes or temptations is making an assault on your family, let God take control and teach your children to do likewise. This begins by humbly calling on God to take over the battle being waged against you. *(Matthew 6: 9, 13)* When God is allowed in, Satan and all of his worldly forces will have to retreat. If you don't call on the Lord, then you will likely lose to those under Satan's control, because as much as Satan is no match for God, neither are you a match against Satan's evil plots and worldly influences.

When the young boy perished at my youth camp, I believe most of us at first thought it was just an unfortunate accident, but as time passed, we became more convinced that this was an assault by Satan. His purpose was clear, to destroy our faith and confidence in God, something he is infamous for doing with others throughout the centuries. The tragic deaths of Job's family in the Old Testament and Stephen's death in the New Testament are two examples of this. *(Acts 7:59-60; Job 1:8-12, 18-22)* However, what Satan tried to do to my youth group didn't work, because we immediately put our trust in God when it happened. When we did, the Lord responded quickly and took over, causing Satan to exit quickly; he has never been able to stand up long against the overwhelming presence of God.

In a like way, put your faith and trust immediately in God when feeling that your family is being assaulted by one of Satan's schemes, tragedies, or even one of his many temptations brought to you by others. Simply say, *"Help Lord!" "Come to my family's rescue!" "Take control!"* And He will!

Use the Sword

In confrontations with worldly influences and practices, encourage your children to learn and memorize the Scripture. If Jesus quoted Scripture and used it to fend off Satan, then your children should strive to do the same as soon as they are old enough to do so. The main reason is that the Scripture will teach them all they need to know about God and life on this earth. With such knowledge and truth in their hearts, along with the presence of the Spirit, there is no temptation the world can present they won't be able to overcome.

Take up the sword of the Spirit, which is the Word of God. (Ephesians 6:17)

When teaching your children the Scriptures, do so with great fervor, for every verse read, studied, or memorized is one more the Holy Spirit can bring to their minds in the course of a battle. *(John 14:26)* He certainly did with several of those in my youth group that tragic weekend, particularly the counselors who were there. Although I can't remember all of the verses the Spirit brought forth from them, here are some that likely surfaced.

"O death, where is your victory? O death, where is your sting?"...but thanks be to God, who gives us the victory through our Lord Jesus Christ. Therefore, my beloved brethren, be steadfast, immovable, always abounding in the work of the Lord, knowing that your toil is not in vain in the Lord. (I Corinthians 15:55, 57-58)

But we do not want you to be uninformed, brethren, about those who are asleep, so that you will not grieve as do the rest who have no hope. For if we believe that Jesus died and rose again, even so God will bring with Him those who have fallen asleep in Jesus. For this we say to you by the word of the Lord, that we, who are alive and remain until the coming of the Lord, will not precede those who have fallen asleep. For the Lord Himself will descend from heaven with a shout, with the voice of the archangel and with the trumpet of God, and the dead in Christ will rise first. Then we who are alive and remain will be caught up together with them in the clouds to meet the Lord in the air, and so we shall always be with the Lord. Therefore comfort one another with these words. (I Thessalonians 4:13-18)

Blessed be the God and Father of our Lord Jesus Christ, the Father of mercies and God of all comfort, who comforts us in all our affliction so that we will be able to comfort those who are in any affliction with the comfort with which we ourselves are comforted by God. (II Corinthians 1:3-4)

Final thoughts

Whether you want to or not, your family needs to develop a relationship with this world, even though at times it can be very evil, gross, and anti-God. You need to because both you and your children are God's avenues to reach this world for His kingdom. For that reason, in the midst of battling the world's various sinful practices, temptations, and perverted beliefs, you cannot lose your desire to see those in the world come to know Jesus as Lord and Savior. After all, the last words Jesus gave to his disciples before leaving for heaven were not to protect themselves from the evils of this world, but rather to go and make disciples of everyone, baptizing them in the name of the Father, Son, and Spirit. *(Matthew 28:19)*

Teachable Moment

In this chapter there are several truths and realities about the world that your family needs to remember if you are going to survive and thrive against its negative influences. In doing so, pick two gated areas you often see, both that can only be entered when the gate is opened or breached. This illustration is akin to what Jesus taught His disciples about the gates of Hades not holding up against their preaching of the Gospel.

Therefore, let one gated area represent where your family lives, which remains locked when attacked by the temptations and values of this world. And let the other gated area represent those living in the world, which are victimized and overrun by the influences of Satan. In respect to this compound, picture your family knocking down its gate with the Gospel, so that all who are within can be saved and set free.

The following verses referenced in this chapter can be found in sequence on my web site, www.tmoments.com. Click on the Book Resources button located on the home page.

Isaiah 14:12; Mark 1:13; Matthew 13:19; Luke 4:3; Isaiah 14:12-17; II Corinthians 11:13; I Timothy 1:3-7; II Timothy 4:1-3; Acts 26:21-28; Matthew 2:13-16; Matthew 4:1-11; Luke 22:31; Luke 22:3; John 21:25; Matthew 5:1-6; Matthew 8:1-3; Luke 8:27-32; Matthew 16:13-16; II Peter 2:4-9; Romans 8:31, 38-39; 1John 10:27-28; Genesis 3:1-6; Job 1: 9, 12 Luke 22:31; Matthew 4:3; Acts 5:3; II Corinthians 7:5; Matthew 6:9, 13; Acts 7:59-60; Job 1:8-12, 18-22; John 14:26; Matthew 28:19

EIGHTEEN
OPENING YOUR GATES
(Equipping your children to win others for Christ)

For I determined to know nothing among you except Jesus Christ, and Him crucified. I was with you in weakness and in fear and in much trembling, and my message and my preaching were not in persuasive words of wisdom, but in demonstration of the Spirit and of power, so that your faith would not rest on the wisdom of men, but on the power of God.

(I Corinthians 2:2-5)

This last chapter on preparing your children for the world deals with the second part of developing a relationship with it, winning those to Christ under its influence. Your family, in addition to all families dedicated to Christ, is in a unique position to do this, because you rub shoulders with those of the world everyday. Some are your neighbors, friends, acquaintances, fellow workers, and even extended family members. Others you buy gas, groceries, or insurance from, and still others are your children's friends, school mates, and teachers. Not sharing Christ with them, and not equipping your children to do likewise one day, constitutes missed opportunities for the kingdom.

To gain a biblical perspective in reaching those enslaved to the world, we will observe the importance Paul put on presenting the Gospel, the responsibility he felt all believers had in respect to this, and the boldness and flexibility he modeled while sharing Christ. Finally, we will review the simplicity of Jesus' salvation message, who He shared it with first, and what He said in regard to finding good candidates for the kingdom.

Paul

According to Paul, one of the most important things Christians should do on earth is to present the Gospel of Christ to others. He felt that if they didn't, then those who hadn't heard might end up lost to the kingdom forever. He stated this in a letter to his fellow believers in Rome.

For the Scripture says, "Whoever believes in Him will not be disappointed." How then will they call on Him in whom they have not believed? How will they believe in Him whom they have not heard? And how will they hear without a preacher? (Romans 10:11, 14)

Paul also felt presenting the Gospel was a responsibility to be shared by all believers, not just himself or other Apostles, preachers, teachers, and gifted evangelists of his day. This is perhaps why he used the pronoun *"we"* so much in his writings, like: *"we are all fellow workers in God's kingdom, we preach Christ crucified, we preach Christ Jesus as Lord, we are a fragrance of Christ to the perishing, and we are ambassadors for Christ making an appeal to others."* This is the same responsibility your family also shares today with other believers, including those who preach, teach, or evangelize on Sunday mornings. *(I Corinthians 3:9; I Corinthians 1:22-23; II Corinthians 4:5; II Corinthians 2:15-17; II Corinthians 5:20)*

In addition to Paul's thoughts and feelings on winning the lost, he was incredibly bold in presenting the Gospel. Several times throughout his ministry, he knowingly risked his own life to share it with others. Sometimes he was beaten with a rod for preaching Christ, at other times he was lashed on the back, dragged out of a city, and even stoned. Because of this and the power of his message, many listened, considered, contemplated, and believed.

Five times I received from the Jews thirty-nine lashes. Three times I was beaten with rods, once I was stoned… (II Corinthians 11:24-25)

What made Paul so bold can only be attributed to his faith in God and the Spirit who always strengthened him during difficult encounters and circumstances. This didn't mean Paul walked into each of these situations without fear or trepidation; he definitely did, as expressed in the following letter to the Corinthian church. Due to his faith and the overwhelming power of the Spirit though, he was able to overcome his apprehension. God will do the same for you and your children as you present the Gospel to others.

And when I came to you, brethren, I did not come with superiority of speech or of wisdom, proclaiming to you the testimony of God. For I determined to know nothing among you except Jesus Christ, and Him crucified. I was with you in weakness and in fear and in much trembling, and my message and my preaching were not in persuasive words of wisdom, but in demonstration of the

Spirit and of power. (I Corinthians 2:1-4)

Lastly, Paul was a great planner when it came to presenting the Word to others. For instance, during a 14 year span, he put together three separate missionary journeys to communities and cities throughout Asia Minor, Greece, and the Mediterranean region. In his fourth and last journey, the Roman government (through the influence of the Lord) did his planning, sending him by ship in chains to Rome, from which he never returned.   In addition to being a good planner, Paul was also very good at *hanging loose,* so to speak, and being flexible to do whatever for whomever God sent his way. Because of his flexibility, God asked Paul to share the Gospel with the Gentiles, to preach in synagogues   with contentious and unbelieving Jews, to debate the intellectuals, to spend time discipling other believers, and to share Christ with the Roman soldiers chained to him during the last days of his life. *(Acts 13:44-49; Acts 19:6-10; Acts 17:22-23; Philippians 1:1-5; Philippians 1:12-15)*

What made Paul such a good planner and yet, so flexible? It wasn't any adequacy he saw in himself, but rather a belief that God could take whatever he planned, or didn't plan, and work it together for the good of the kingdom. He will do the same for your family if you simply commit to sharing Christ with whomever God sends your way.

And we know that God causes all things to work together for good to those who love God, to those who are called according to His purpose. (Romans 8:28)

Jesus

Jesus did many things as He shared the Gospel, but three of the most important were: keeping His message simple, prioritizing who to give it to first, and analyzing the response after presenting the truth.

First, Jesus' teachings on salvation were simple, uncomplicated, and straight forward. Essentially, He taught that if you wanted to have a relationship with God, then all you needed to do was repent and admit your sins to God, ask for His forgiveness, and believe that He, Jesus, was the Son of God who took the guilt of those sins upon Himself at the cross. Jesus went on to teach that after making such a confession and declaration, God would then enter your life through the Spirit to help you live out the remainder of it according to His will. At the end, when your time was up on earth, God, Himself, would usher you into heaven.

(I Thessalonians 4:14) In heaven you would experience an indescribable and unparalleled life with Him and others, filled with boundless love, joy, peace, and unending purpose.

When preparing your children to share the salvation message, focus on the following basic and simple truths.

Man's sinfulness

If we say that we have no sin, we are deceiving ourselves and the truth is not in us. If we confess our sins, He is faithful and righteous to forgive us our sins and to cleanse us from all unrighteousness. (I John 1:8-9)

Repentance, belief, and forgiveness:

...Jesus came into Galilee, preaching the gospel of God, saying, "The time is fulfilled, and the kingdom of God is at hand; repent and believe in the gospel." (Mark 1:14-15)

If you confess with your mouth Jesus as Lord, and believe in your heart that God raised Him from the dead, you will be saved; for with the heart a person believes, resulting in righteousness, and with the mouth he confesses, resulting in salvation. (Romans 10: 9-10)

God's entrance and help

"I (Jesus) will ask the Father, and He will give you another Helper (Holy Spirit), that He may be with you forever." (John 14:16)

...the love of God has been poured out within our hearts through the Holy Spirit who was given to us. (Romans 5:5)

Promise of heaven

"In My Father's house are many dwelling places; if it were not so, I would have told you; for I go to prepare a place for you. If I go and prepare a place for you, I will come again and receive you to Myself, that where I am, there you may be also". (John 14:2-3)

The Jews were Jesus' first priority when sharing salvation. God (Father,

Spirit, and Son) likely wanted to give them another chance to do what He had asked them to do centuries before, which was to be His light and representatives to the world. In this, Israel, whom God called His first born, was to share with those in the world who God was, what life should be like, and how they could gain a relationship with Him. With a few exceptions, and a few periods of time when they trusted Him, Israel did none of what God asked. Thus when Christ began His public ministry, He started with Israel once again, teaching them how to live their lives unto God so that the world could be reached. While Jesus did this, He also reached out to those who weren't Jews, like the Gentiles, Greeks, Romans, and Samaritans. *(Matthew 15:23-28; Matthew 8:8, 10-11; John 4:39-42)* Of course, Israel, for the most part, once again, didn't respond but crucified Him instead.

After Jesus' resurrection, God took Israel's representative role and gave it to the church, his second born so to speak. Unlike Israel, the church would be made up of all believers regardless of background or nationality. *(Romans 1:16)* In response, the church, although not perfect, has done its job, for today there are more people in the world who know God and have received His salvation than ever before. To prepare your children to present the Gospel, you might start out first with those in your extended family as God did with the Jews (Israel). If there is little or no response, move onto others who are more receptive to the Gospel. They, as the church became to God, will likely end up to be the family for which you had hoped.

To help us see who might be a good prospect for the kingdom of God, Jesus gave a simple illustration that presented the basics of what to look for in others.

When a large crowd was coming together, and those from the various cities were journeying to Him, He spoke by way of a parable: "The sower went out to sow his seed; and as he sowed, some fell beside the road, and it was trampled under foot and the birds of the air ate it up. Other seed fell on rocky soil, and as soon as it grew up, it withered away, because it had no moisture. Other seed fell among the thorns; and the thorns grew up with it and choked it out. Other seed fell into the good soil, and grew up, and produced a crop a hundred times as great." As He said these things, He would call out, "He, who has ears to hear, let him hear." His disciples began questioning Him as to what this parable meant. "Now the parable is this: the seed is the word of God. Those beside the road are those who have heard; then the devil comes and takes away the word from their heart, so that they will not believe and be saved. Those on the rocky soil are those who, when they hear, receive the word with joy; and these have no firm root; they believe for a while, and in time of temptation fall away. The seed which fell among the thorns, these are the ones who have heard, and as they go on their way they are choked with worries and riches and pleasures of this life, and bring no fruit to maturity. But the seed in the good soil, these are the ones who have heard the word in an honest and good heart, and hold it fast, and bear fruit with perseverance." (Luke 8:4-8, 11-15)

Jesus taught in this parable to share the message of salvation to everyone, not withholding it from any. Then wait and see what the response is, which could be: out and out rejection (*seeds on the road*), immediate interest, but no acceptance (*seeds in the rocks*), seeming acceptance, but eventual abandonment (*seeds amongst the thorns*), and genuine acceptance (*seeds in good soil*).

Jesus sometimes gave the salvation message to the same people over and over again, for many followed him from place to place. You should do the same with your extended family if they don't believe right away, for often it takes more than one presentation to take root. The sower in Jesus' parable wouldn't have given up on a plot of ground just because it didn't instantly sprout; he would have watered and weeded it for awhile until it had a chance to produce.

Parent Application

To prepare your children to reach this fallen world for Christ here are some points and applications to consider under these headings: *Opening Your Gates, Being Bold, Planning and Being Flexible, Sharing the Gospel with the Extended Family,* and *Guarding the Gates.*

Opening Your Gates

At the end of the previous chapter a challenge was given to do more than protect your children from the negative influences of this world, but to also reach out to those in it with the Gospel. The core lesson behind doing this was Jesus' teaching to the disciples: *The gates of hell (Satan's influence) will not prevail against you when you do.* Today, this calls for all believers, including your family, to take the Gospel of Christ to those in the world who are trapped behind the gates of Satan's influence and domination. The best way your family can do this is to open the gates of your own home to others; that is, to make it a place where they can find God, salvation, and the great truths of Scripture. If you do this, then there's no telling who or how many God will send your way to be won over.

Being Bold

To share Christ with others, it's important to be confident and bold about Christ, because if you're not, then those you're trying to reach likely won't take you seriously.   Paul, as you saw, was a great example of boldness, for his willingness to risk his life before others eventually brought many to Christ. Acquiring a similar kind of boldness is possible for everyone, because it's a quality God gives to you when you pray and depend on His strength. *(Ephesians 6:18-20)*

In respect to my family, there was one situation where boldness played out well. It didn't come with me, my wife, or my typically gutsy little daughter, but from my nine- year-old son. In this incident, Brodie's boldness not only got through to a neighbor boy but to his parents, as well. Now, let me say from the top that what Brodie did didn't bring them to Christ, but it certainly got them thinking and interested in Christ and the Christian life.

Sam was a neighborhood boy who my son Brodie played with from time to time, but it wasn't until they were both on the same basketball team in our city sports program that they became good friends. A coach was needed for the team, so I volunteered because I loved being near my son during his sports. One of the other boy's fathers also volunteered to be my assistant. Our little team did pretty well, winning most of its games and making the playoffs. During the playoffs, we won all of our first round games, making it to the semifinals. There was a rule that had to be observed by all teams in which every kid had to play so many quarters of each game. Right before our semifinal game, I wasn't able to make the last practice, so my assistant coach took over. Somehow, during that practice, he was able to get Sam to quit. Now, that was an advantage to our team because although Sam was a good athlete in other sports, basketball was not his forte. Without Sam in our rotation, as our assistant coach must have figured, our chances of winning the championship game were pretty good. Before deciding how to handle this as the coach, I decided to include Brodie in the decision process.

Before saying anything I let Brodie talk. He immediately said that Sam needed to be brought back on the team that winning wasn't everything. I agreed, and called Sam's house, but his parents were reluctant to talk with me, thinking I was part of what happened. I could have dropped things right there, but before I could speak, Brodie said he would go over to Sam's and talk him out of quitting. After we prayed together, that is exactly what he did. As a result, Sam was overcome by Brodie's care and boldness, so he rejoined the team. We barely lost the game and wound up in third place. It didn't matter though, because both Brodie and I felt what we did brought this neighbor family a little closer to the kingdom of God. They even talked of visiting the church I pastored, but they never did. Maybe one day, we will run across them again, and find that they finally accepted Christ. The point is that you do all you can to bring others into the kingdom, which sometimes means being bold and doing what's right for the sake of another.

Planning and Being Flexible

When my wife and I started ministering together, we always planned to make our home open to others. This began by having young people over during our first youth ministry and continued even when we had our own children. However, in the midst of letting people come into our home, God always surprised us with some we hadn't planned for, as He did with Paul throughout his missionary journeys. Several who came to our home were older and in different stages of life than Myrna and I. Sadly, others were victims of abuse, rejection, sickness, and broken relationships. There were even those who showed up on our doorsteps who were sinners in almost every category of life, even victimizers and abusers of others. I actually had to drive one to jail one evening to finish off his sentence. No matter, we didn't turn any away, but tried to do our best to either lead them to Christ or teach them from the Word. For that reason, it is important to keep flexibility in mind if you plan on opening up your home to minister to others. If you do, both you and your children will benefit as you learn how to present the Gospel.

Sharing the Gospel with the Extended Family

You may have extended family who believes in Christ; if so, then all the better for your family, especially when you spend special holidays together like Christmas and Easter. If you have grandparents, aunts, uncles, and cousins who don't believe in Christ, or haven't accepted Him as Lord and Savior, make them a priority, just as Jesus did with the Jews and His own earthly family before beginning His public ministry. When presenting the Gospel, pick opportune times to do so, rather than hammering them over the head with it every time you get together. In the in-between times, love and accept them as Christ would if He were in your place. Sometimes, this loving relationship speaks louder to them than a powerful and convincing argument.

In our family, we have had both those who took hold of Christ and those who didn't. For those who didn't, we often prayed for them, speaking of our faith when appropriate, and living the Christian life in their presence as best we could. As time passed, several came to accept Christ through the testimonies of others. We were thrilled for them.

Guarding the Gates

In Jesus' day, many of the large cities had guards at the main gates to make sure no one entered who might cause trouble or havoc. In like manner, when you open up the gates of your home to others, especially the neighborhood kids and school mates, you need to keep a careful watch on them. This does not mean you keep children out of your home who aren't Christians, but you might keep them out if their influence starts to overpower your children's beliefs or behavior.

When our kids were young, we had a few instances where Myrna and I had to carefully watch over Brodie and Shannon's friends. With a few of them, we simply didn't let our children go over to their homes or be alone with them. These kids were allowed to come to our home, but not the other way around. Eventually, Brodie and Shannon lost contact with these kids, but not before we as a family modeled the Christian life to them. You may experience some of the same in regards to your own children's friends. Hang in there, and pray they come to know the Lord through your influence.

Final Comments

Finally, I want to make one last mention of the kids in my Seattle youth group, particularly those who later became parents. Several opened up their homes to share Christ with others. Because they did, many were reached who would not have been otherwise, and perhaps more importantly, their own children's faith was strengthened by doing so. Now these children have grown up, are marrying, and beginning to have families of their own. Not surprisingly, they, like their parents, also have a desire to open their homes to others. So, what started off as a tragedy in a weekend camp so many years ago, where so many young people dedicated their lives to Christ, has now worked itself into quite a ministry that keeps adding and adding and adding to the kingdom.

Teachable Moments

To remember one of the main thrusts of this chapter, which is to make your home a place where those in the world can find God, locate a port, dock, or boat launch. If this isn't possible, then look for one on T.V, the internet, or in a book. Take note of the boats coming and going; they are like those in the world who are seeking a spiritual place to land. You are that port, dock, or launch, in that you provide for them a place where they can learn of Christ's offer of salvation and all that pertains to life according to the Scriptures. When the port, dock, or launch is open for business, it's like you're saying to others that you are ready and willing to share God's truth with them. The next time you or your entire family see such a port, dock, or boat launch, let it remind you of the world's search for a Savior and your role and willingness to help them find Him.

The following verses referenced in this chapter can be found in sequence on my web site, www.tmoments.com. Click on the Book Resources button located on the home page.

I Corinthians 3:9; I Corinthians 1:22-23; II Corinthians 4:5; II Corinthians 2:15-17; II Corinthians 5:20; Acts 13:44-49; Acts 19:6-10; Acts 17:22-23; Philippians 1:1-5; Philippians 1:12-15; I Thessalonians 4:14; Matthew 15:23-28; Matthew 8:8, 10-11; John 4:39-42; Romans 1: 16; Ephesians 6:18-20

CONCLUSION

(Preparing for your children's leaving)

"My Spirit which is upon you and My words which I have put in your mouth shall not depart from your mouth, nor from the mouth of your offspring, nor from the mouth of your offspring's offspring," says the LORD, *"from now and forever."*
(Isaiah 59:21)

Before you move onto the Teachable Moment's companion book, *Sowing Teachable Moments Year One*, let me leave you with some final comments on parenting.

No matter how old your children are at the moment, you must realize that one day they will leave to establish a life, family, and home of their own. How you relate to them now, as well as in the years to come, will greatly impact their ability to be all they can be in God's eyes as single adults, husbands and wives, and even parents themselves.

I have found that one of the most difficult challenges in parenting was letting my children go after spending so many years together with them. Although my wife and I were very sad to see them go, both our children felt confident and prepared in the Lord to do so.

I'll never forget coming home from work the day after my daughter Shannon went off to college. She was the last of my children to leave the roost. I looked around the house, walked into her bedroom, noticed how clean it was for a change, stared at the walls, and then said to my wife as she walked in, "Shannon's gone; she's really gone. So what do we do now; what do we do in such an empty house?" Myrna said nothing. She shrugged her shoulders and walked out, for she had been dwelling on the same thought all day.

Perhaps, you will have a different reaction when your children leave; maybe it will be one of relief or even a sense of freedom. No matter your reaction to your children's departure, it is important how you prepare yourself and them for their leaving, particularly in respect to your continuing relationship. The Scripture has given perspective on this with Paul's relationship to Timothy and Jesus' letting go of His disciples when it was time.

Paul

As you help prepare your children for leaving, one of the best models to consider is Paul and his ministry to young Timothy, one of his most devoted disciples. Paul was very close to Timothy, often calling him a son, one of his children, and even a brother. *(I Timothy 1:1-2; I Timothy 1:18; Romans 16:21)* In Paul's discipleship of Timothy, he spent a great deal of time at the beginning teaching him the Word and working hand-in-hand with him in ministry. This all came to a close when Paul left, leaving Timothy alone to carry out God's will. So it should be the same with your children, as they need to one day walk with God and do His will apart from you.

As painful as it must have been for Paul to leave Timothy, it was for Timothy's good, as well as the spread of the Gospel. To have another in the world preaching the Word as Paul had been doing could only help the cause of Christ all the more. Paul's separation from Timothy also gave him the time and opportunity to disciple others.

During Paul's separation from Timothy, his love and concern never faded; he was not an out-of-sight, out-of-mind person. This was shown through the letters Paul wrote to Timothy. In one letter for instance, he spoke of his non-stop prayers for Timothy, his longing to see him again, and the joy he felt when they were together. In another, he applauded Timothy's faith and recalled the tears Timothy shed when they were together.

For this reason I have sent to you Timothy, who is my beloved and faithful child in the Lord, and he will remind you of my ways which are in Christ, just as I teach everywhere in every church. (I Corinthians 4:17)

To Timothy, my beloved son: grace, mercy and peace from God the Father and Christ Jesus our Lord. I thank God, whom I serve with a clear conscience the way my forefathers did, as I constantly remember you in my prayers night and day, longing to see you, even as I recall your tears, so that I may be filled with joy. For I am mindful of the sincere faith within you, which first dwelt in your grandmother Lois and your mother Eunice, and I am sure that it is in you as well. (II Timothy 1:2-5)

Not long after the thoughts in this letter were written, Paul was executed for his faith in Rome, never to see Timothy again on earth. Yet, their bond during those last days couldn't have been greater; their separation from one another never affected that. Similarly, after getting your children ready for this world, your love for them should never change but only become greater after they have left.

Jesus

Jesus' experience with His disciples, whom He considered family and friends, was even greater than Paul's. *(Matthew 12: 48-50; John 15: 13-15)* In His time with them, Jesus did several things applicable to parenting: He spent as much time with His disciples as possible, He listened to their questions, answered their concerns, absolved their fears, taught them truth, and showed them how to live and minister in a very dangerous and tumultuous world. *(Matthew 17:9-10; Matthew 6: 31-32; Luke 24:36-39; Matthew 5:1, 14-16; Matthew 21:18-22)* Most importantly, perhaps, He let them go when it was time to do so, separating Himself from them. *(John 16: 16; Acts 1:9-11)* Jesus did this because He could look into the future and see this was best for their spiritual development, as well as the world's, which was in desperate need of their help and testimony. You need to have the same perspective and resolve with your children, for how will they mature and reach the world themselves if you don't let them go into that world?

Before leaving them, Jesus made the disciples some important promises; He told them they would always be in His thoughts, never be deserted, and would be helped by the Spirit who was being sent. *(Hebrews 13:5; John 14:26)* Hopefully, this grabs your attention, especially in respect to preparing your children for the day when you must let them go. Remember, it was never in Jesus' plan to keep them together with Him for the rest of their earthly lives. Neither should it be for you with your children, but until that day of parting comes, always be there for your children, talk to them, and reassure them.

Parent Application

To prepare your children for leaving, several principles and suggestions come to mind, some from Paul and Jesus, others drawn from personal experience and observation. All fall under the following headings: *Letting Go, Readying Yourself for Their Leaving, Preparing Your Children for that Day,* and *Staying with Them in Spirit.*

Letting Go

Letting go of your kids is a process which begins by understanding what goes on in the heart of parents who refuse to do so, even after their children have married and have kids of their own. Usually, these parents don't let go because they can't bear the thought of not having their kids around as they once did. They fight the separation because their children filled so many of their own personal needs; they had someone to talk to, disciple, fellowship with, and rule over. The idea of starting over with others after their kids have left is too uncomfortable, awkward, and requires too much effort. Therefore, instead of doing what they should, they hang onto their kids making them feel guilty about not coming around or including them in what they are doing

I have seen parents like these try to limit their kids' relationships with others after leaving. Some refuse to let their grown children bring friends home for special holidays, such as Christmas, Thanksgiving, or birthdays. They did this because they didn't want their children to have special times with anyone else except themselves. The idea of reaching out to others didn't register to them. Their love for themselves outweighed their responsibility to love and include others.

Other parents with whom I have worked struggled to let their kids go because they didn't want their patriarchal or matriarchal leadership roles diminished or lessened with their children. These roles are important when raising children, but they need to take a back seat after their children have grown up. *(Proverbs 6:20-23)* Tearfully, some of these parents lost contact with their kids over the years due to the constant pressure they put on their grown children, resulting in the very opposite of what they had hoped. Other parents ended up deterring their children from reaching out to others, the very opposite of what the Scriptures teach.

In view of this, if you believe you may have a tendency toward these attitudes, take a long hard look at the way Christ prepared His disciples, and then follow His example and do the same with your children. He spent a lot of time developing a close relationship with His disciples during their early years together, but when it came time to let them go, He let them go. In fact, He removed Himself from them so they would have no choice but to move on and do for others what He had done for them. Do likewise and you won't regret it, not only in the short run but the long run as well.

Readying Yourself for Their Leaving

Have more children

Next in the process of letting go is what you can do to ready yourself for this coming transition, which will arrive before you know it. I still can't believe the time my wife and I had with our kids is over. So, if you believe you are going to struggle with letting go because you won't have any kids to take care of any longer, then have a slew of them to extend your time as a parent. The Scripture speaks highly of having many children, even if our present society sort of looks down upon it now. I have some friends who have had ten or more children; others have had five or six. My wife and I only had two, not because we didn't want more, but because it would have been physically dangerous for Myrna.

Adopting children or opening your home to children in foster care not only meets a growing need in our culture, it also allows you to continue parenting. Children in foster care and in need of adoption certainly need all the love and support parents like you can give them. More importantly, they need the Lord in their lives.

In watching our friends who had several children, none seemed to struggle with letting each of their children go when it was time. Their advantage was that when one was about to leave the roost, another was on his or her way. By the time all the kids had been raised, these friends were pretty exhausted. However, filling the void they may have felt were a host of grandchildren on the way. So having many children helps in the process of letting your children go when it's time. I'm sure there are better and even more important reasons for having many children, for God says blessed is the man whose quiver is full.

Behold, children are a gift of the Lord, the fruit of the womb is a reward. Like arrows in the hand of a warrior, so are the children of one's youth. How blessed is the man whose quiver is full of them. (Psalm 127:3-5)

Minister to another's children

If having more children is not feasible but continually being with children is, then begin working with other children even while raising your own. In fact, include your own children in the process; it will

191

teach your kids how to minister and reach out to others. Children's programs at church or in a local Christian school are great places where you can plug in and do this. In my experience as a Children's Pastor and a Christian School Administrator, I have met many parents who did this. As a result, when it came time for their kids to leave home, they handled it well. Instead of trying to hold on, they invested themselves even more into the children in the programs, especially with the kids who didn't have good homes or supportive parents.

Because these parents did this, they very much lived out the principle Paul demonstrated with Timothy, in that when his time with Timothy was finished, he moved onto others who needed discipling. If you choose this path, you can begin now or as soon as your children are old enough to join and assist you.

Develop other friendships

I have found it important to form friendships with my children as they grew older, especially as they approached adulthood. A friend is someone I trust, have fun with, supports me through thick and thin, is easy to talk with on any subject, and can accept my bad points along with the good. As much as I encourage you to develop such a friendship with your children, I caution you not to make them your only friends as I have seen some parents do. Your children, like you, need other friendships to help them mature in the Lord. If both parent and child develop outside friendships and relationships, it will greatly benefit all of you as the parting approaches, for it will give you others to which you can turn.

Preparing Your Children for that Day

Help them discover who they should be

Helping your children discover who they are in the Lord, and what they are called to be and do, may be your greatest contribution in getting them ready for the day of their leaving. This begins early on by encouraging them to develop their own personalities, thinking, values, skills, and ways of doing things. Even though the Lord gave you the responsibility of raising your children, it was not His intention to make them carbon copies of you or to fulfill your dreams. The varying personalities, spiritual gifts, and calls to ministry throughout Scripture are proof of this. Even the disciples who were carefully nurtured by Jesus Himself hardly resembled each other when He was done with them. Each had his own unique distinctiveness, giftedness, and call, as your children should when they strike out on their own. The more you have this in mind, the more confident they will be in themselves, because they will be living out the particular desires and dreams God gave to them. If you try to force your dreams and aspirations on your children, you are likely to hinder, rather than help them make a good transition from your home. Remember, your job of discipleship is to help your children become like Christ and Him alone. *(I John 3:2; Ephesians 5:1)*

Decreasing your control

Lastly, and perhaps the most difficult in the process of letting go, is lessening your control and authority over them as that time approaches. In the Scripture, John the Baptist's closing days of his ministry are a picture of this. For years he was the dominant figure bringing truth to the Jewish people, but when Jesus arrived, he knew it was time to take a back seat to Him. He even said, *"I must decrease now, so that Jesus may increase." (John 3:29-30)* In principle you need to do the same as your children grow older; your control over them needs to decrease. You do so because you want them to be able to handle any challenges the world brings. Is this not what you wanted for yourself when you were young? Should it be any different for your children? Besides, is this not what the Lord wants for them, children who can walk away from their home ready and willing to serve Him in any capacity anywhere in the world?

My wife and I certainly decreased our control over our kids as they got older, particularly when they approached young adulthood. Two situations come to mind with my son: one when he was almost sixteen and the other a year later when a senior in high school. In the first situation, he was working for me at Lake Almanor, a place where we had a cabin and vacationed every summer. I was the recreation director there each summer, which was a nice break from teaching school. Brodie was one of my lifeguards, which not only gave him a decent income, but also the opportunity to meet a number of pretty girls on the beach (as he saw it). Get the picture? Now, this latter benefit didn't bother me much because I trusted Brodie's character. He had been consistently devoted to the ideals of his church youth group back at home, as well as to his relationship with the Lord. However, one night we really got into a debate with one another into the wee hours of the morning over his freedom. In our talk, Brodie felt that since he had been so faithful to the Lord, he should be given the freedom to come in anytime he wanted. I disagreed and maintained he keep the curfew my wife and I had set for him. In the midst of our back and forth exchanges, I complimented him for his faith, but explained he was not yet ready for all the temptations awaiting him in the world. He vehemently disagreed but finally accepted my judgment on the matter.

A year later in a second much shorter conversation, I gave Brodie the freedom he wanted. This lessened my control over him, but it was the right thing to do because he was more mature and ready spiritually. On a side note, in one of my journals I ran across the other day describing these events, I noted that Brodie told me years later I was right to refuse him the freedom he was seeking in our first go around. Evidently, much of his argument was motivated more from the desire to see and say good-by to a girl he met on the beach, one who was leaving the next day for home.

If your children are young and the day of their leaving seems far off, I understand, for both my wife and I were once where you are. I only wish we were there again, because raising Brodie and Shannon went far too quickly for us. But no matter, before the time comes to give your children their freedom, I suggest doing a couple of things. First, allow them to spend time at friend's homes where they can experience a degree of being on their own. Of course you will have to be careful at which friend's home you allow them to spend time; not all homes are safe. Some may have parents who are not responsible, while others have children in the home who are bad influences. Second, as your children get older, allow them more and more freedom to go to events outside of your home. Schoolmate parties, Sunday school outings, or trips with a team they may be on, are some to consider. In each of these situations, as well as many others like them, you are not present. This is important because in a small way it helps your children handle life only with God and what you've taught them. The more you do this, from one situation and age level to the next, the better equipped they (and you) will be when that time comes for them to leave home for good and forge their way in the world.

Staying with Them in Spirit

Myrna and I loved our children; we got along well with them even after they became young adults. Amazingly, we saw *eye-to-eye* on most issues, which is not typical even in Christian families. I believe if they had not been our children, they would have been close friends. Regardless of this relationship, we never pushed them to live near home after growing up. Instead, we wanted them to be where God wanted them, even if that was far from us. Even after my son and his wife had children, we didn't try to convince them to move closer so we could help raise their kids. We loved the idea of helping, of course, and certainly did when asked, but God showed us through time and circumstance that they needed to do this for themselves. Thus, in our situation not being around the corner was the best way to accomplish this.

We still keep in close contact with our kids and their families, as I believe Paul did in principle with Timothy and others. For just as he wrote letters and sent messages to those he loved and longed to see; my wife and I have done the same with our kids by visiting, calling, emailing, and writing them letters. In my letters and emails, I sometimes remind them of the past times we had together, especially those experiences with the Lord. I was able to recall these because I had written them down in my journals.

One year at Christmas, I gave them each a family devotional to always have and use with their families. In it were favorite verses, sayings, and pictures of them growing up. Here is the beginning excerpt that appeared on the first page of this family devotional.

Dear Brodie and Shannon,

Over the last two and a half years, I have worked on a family devotional which I am passing onto you and your family. In putting this devotional together I read the Bible from cover to cover picking and organizing favorite verses and meaningful passages. This devotional book is broken up into two divisions.

The first represents two months of daily readings each which include quotes from different Christian writers and various verses and passages. On each page there are old pictures of our family to remind you of the wonderful times we had together.

The second division includes thirty-three different subject areas with the same format; I have found this section particularly helpful when counseling others, as I hope you will also. They are under the headings: Anger, Character/

Humility, Children, Comfort, Commitment, Confession, Confidence, Courage, Criticism, Discipleship, Leadership, Encouragement, Enemy/ Satan, Faithfulness, Grace, Heaven, His Will, Loss, Love, Our Strength, Our Words, Our Works, Perseverance, Perspective, Prayer/Praise, Reward/ Victory, Righteousness, Sin, Trials/Temptations, Unity, Walking in the Spirit, Winning Others, Wisdom/Knowledge, and Worry.

Merry Christmas,
Dad

Perhaps, one day you might do something similar to keep your kids close to you in spirit, and in the Spirit. If you want to do such a devotional; I can help. On my web site (*www.tmoments.com*) under the heading *Family Devotionals* are the sayings and verses I used. All you have to do is paste in your own pictures at the top of each page, print it, and put it in a folder that displays your family name and picture.

Final Thoughts

The book of Ecclesiastes teaches there is a time for everything under the sun and that includes the phases of parenting. *(Ecclesiastes 3:1-2)* There is a time to pour yourself into your children when they are young, and there is a time to back away and let them go after they have grown up. There is a time to lead them, and there is a time to serve them when they are having families of their own. Lastly, there is a time to play the role of patriarch or matriarch of the family, and there is a time to step away and give that over to your children.

Last Teachable Moment

Years ago, when dropping our son off at college for his freshman year, it was quite memorable and emotional to say the least. In preparation for this, my wife and I helped pack his suitcases, bought him the basics on which to live, and then drove two days to get him to school. During the drive, I was quite controlled and contained, Myrna was less so, but my son Brodie was thrilled and excited about what lay ahead. After arriving, we drove around the school and then dropped by one of the stores to buy a few extra things for him. We eventually made our way over to his dorm and unpacked. After getting Brodie settled in, we went down to the car to say our goodbyes. After climbing into the car, each of us prayed, but as I prayed my voice cracked a bit and tears began to flow. I think Brodie and my wife were surprised, and so was I to tell you the truth, but leaving him that day weighed heavy on my heart. However, we did leave him, and as time proved, letting him go was not only the best for him, it was for us, as well. He went on to do some great things for the Lord at school, and we went back home to pour ourselves into our daughter who was still in high school. Later, after college was done, both of our kids established careers, married, and set up Christian homes of their own.

For this Teachable Moment, pause from time to time and look at your children's faces, picturing the day they will leave and strike out on their own. As you look intently into their eyes, say to yourself, "I love you and will do all I can to ready you for that day. I will disciple you, teach you God's Word, and be the example the Lord wants me to be as your parent." Then, picture yourself driving off as we did that day with Brodie; tearful, yet content with who your children have become and what they will do in this life.

The following verses referenced in this chapter can be found in sequence on my web site, www.tmoments.com. Click on the Book Resources button located on the home page.

I Timothy 1:1-2; I Timothy 1:18; Romans 16:21; Matthew 12:48-50; John 15:13-15; Matthew 17: 9-10; Matthew 6:31-32; Luke 24:36-39; Matthew 5:1,14-16; Matthew 21:18-22; John 16:16; Acts 1: 9-11; Hebrews 13:5; John 14:26; Proverbs 6:20-23; I John 3:2; Ephesians 5:1; John 3:29-30; Ecclesiastes 3:1-2

EPILOGUE

(Letters to remember)

You are our letter, written in our hearts, known and read by all men; being manifested that you are a letter of Christ, cared for by us, written not with ink but with the Spirit of the living God, not on tablets of stone but on tablets of human hearts.
(II Corinthians 3:2-3)

After reading Teachable Moments, my hope is that you can use some of what has been written to help you raise children who love God, love you, and love others. This was certainly the goal Myrna and I had when we first became parents. Needless to say as you can surmise, we didn't do everything perfectly, nor did we do everything suggested in this book, but we tried. Because of this and what God did in response, both Brodie and Shannon trusted the Lord while growing up and still do today.

Before I wrap up Teachable Moments, let me encourage you to go to my web site (*www.tmoments.com*) and see what else I have there that can help you. Of course, I want to hear from you when you do, particularly if you have created any Teachable Moments on your own that I can pass on to other parents. And if you have any questions about parenting, I'll try and answer them as best I can.

Finally, I leave with you two excerpts from letters written to Myrna and me when our kids were on their own for the first time, both in very secular colleges. As you can imagine these letters warmed our hearts when we read them, but more than that, they validated for us what God and His Word can do when remembered and embedded in the heart.

Dear Dad, (Written by Shannon during her junior year at the University of Arizona)

I know you are praying for me each day and I can't think of a more precious gift than that. I really enjoyed our times together this summer. You made my summer wonderful and I felt like you helped me in so many ways. I miss your words of wisdom and your daily encouragement. God has blessed me so much by allowing me to be your daughter. Who I am today is a reflection of all the wonderful things that you have taught me. You have been there to pep me up when I am down, and let me cry on your shoulder. I have loved our relationship and I feel God was a part of it all. I will always be your spunky slightly tempered girl who loves her father and values his opinions greatly. Nothing will change that. Thank you for all your love and time. Your strength, prayers and love help me get through each day here at school.

Love your little Tom Boy,

Shannon

Dear Mom, *(Written by Brodie at Washington State University, in reference to missing Myrna's birthday)*

Well, I write to inform you, sadly, that I did indeed forget to call you on your birthday and am sorry. It seems to me that I can somehow remember the seemingly meaningless things in life, but not the big things like your birthday.

In all honesty I wanted to write and tell you this last semester, but this provides me with even a better opportunity to let you know just how awesome you have been in my life and are today as well. So believe me when I say that this comes purely from my heart, that when I look back at my life I have only God to thank for Him divinely placing you in my life.

I can hardly think of the word love without thinking about how you have loved me over these last 21 years. True love always verifies itself in action, and every time you tucked me into bed, or called me, or said goodbye you always said, "I love you." But that wasn't the amazing part. The part that drives me is this, behind those three words were hours and hours and years and decades of time in which you showed me you loved me. I remember you in my classroom at school and at the soccer fields and basketball games and plays and concerts and gym days and every hotel pool where I made you watch me dive 50 times.

To pack a lifetime of memories onto a sheet of paper like this is impossible, that's why every day this week I pray that you realize what God has accomplished through you in my life. I wouldn't have made it, mom, no way. And that's why God put you in my life, because He knew what I needed when you chose to follow Him, a plan for you that included me. If I can leave you with one thing, let it be that I will always try and remember from here on every single act of your love, all 2,385,756 of them.

Love your son,

Brodie

NOTES

Chapter 1

1. Kent McClain, *Mission Possible* (Sylmar, California, K.M. Publishing, 1992), pages 1-132. www.tmoments.com.

Chapter 3

1. Dr. Lockyer, *All the Parables of the Bible* (Grand Rapids, Michigan: Zondervan Publishing House, 1963), pages 143-256.
2. Dr. Ray Vander Laan, Edited by Allan Spiers and Paul Varum, *The True Easter Story Tape* (Grand Rapids, Michigan: Zondervan Publishing House; Colorado Springs, Colorado, Focus on the Family, 1996).
3. Dr. Ray Vander Laan, Edited by Allan Spiers and Paul Varum, *The True Easter Story Tape* (Grand Rapids, Michigan: Zondervan Publishing House; Colorado Springs, Colorado, Focus on the Family, 1996).

Chapter 4

1. Ray C. Stedman, *Body Life* (Discovery House Publishers, Grand Rapids, Michigan 1972), pages 200-204.
2. W.E.Vine, *An Expository Dictionary of New Testament Words* (Fleming H. Revell Company, Old Tappan, New Jersey, 1966), pages 20-22.

Chapter 5

1. Dr. Lynn Anderson, *They Smell Like Sheep: Volume 1* (New York: Howard Books, A Division of Simon and Schuster, 1997), pages 19-20.
2. Fred H. Wight, *Manners and Customs of Bible Lands* (Chicago: Moody Press, 1953), page 161.
3. Phillip Keller, *A Shepherd looks at Shepherding* {*Large Print*} (Grand Rapids, Michigan: Zondervan Publishing House, 1970), page 99.
4. David Roper, *The Son of a Passionate Heart 23rd Psalm* (Grand Rapids, Michigan: Discovery Publishing House, 1994), page 28.

Chapter 6

1. Dr. Lynn Anderson, *They Smell Like Sheep: Volume 1* (New York: Howard Books, A Division of Simon and Schuster, 1997), pages 20.
2. Phillip Keller, *A Shepherd looks at Shepherding* {*Large Print*} (Grand Rapids, Michigan: Zondervan Publishing House, 1970), page 35.

Chapter 7

1. Phillip Keller, *A Shepherd looks at Shepherding* {*Large Print*} (Grand Rapids, Michigan: Zondervan Publishing House, 1970), page 35.
2. Dr. Lynn Anderson, They *Smell Like Sheep: Volume 1* (New York: Howard Books, A Division of Simon and Schuster, 1997), page 20.
3. Fred H. Wight, *Manners and Customs of Bible Lands* (Chicago: Moody Press, 1953), page 151.

Chapter 8

1. W.E. Vine, An *Expository Dictionary of New Testament Words: Volume* III (Old Tappan, New Jersey: Fleming H. Revell Company, 1966), page 20-22.

2. Dennis and Barbara Rainey, *Parenting Today's Adolescence* (Nashville, Tennessee: Thomas Nelson Publishers, 1998), pages 19-22.

Chapter 9

1. Phillip Keller, *A Shepherd looks at Psalm 23 {Large Print}* (Grand Rapids, Michigan: Zondervan Publishing House, 1970), page 93.
2. Fred H. Wight, Manners and Customs of Bible Lands (Chicago: Moody Press, 1953), page 149.
3. Fred H. Wight, Manners and Customs of Bible Lands (Chicago: Moody Press, 1953), page 157.
4. Phillip Keller, *A Shepherd looks at Psalm 23* {Large Print} (Grand Rapids, Michigan: Zondervan Publishing House, 1970), pages 93-96.
5. Mrs. Charles E. Cowan, *Steams in the Desert: Volume II* (United States: Cowan Publishing Company, Inc., 1966), September 22nd.
6. Phillip Keller, *A Shepherd looks at Psalm 23 {Large Print}* (Grand Rapids, Michigan: Zondervan Publishing House, 1970), page 95-98.
7. Robert Gamble, *Shepherd My Sheep* (Ireland/Greenville South Carolina: Ambassador Publications Belfast Northern, 1997), pages 88-89.
8. Fred H. Wight, *Manners and Customs of Bible Lands* (Chicago: Moody Press, 1953), pages 150, 156.
9. Mrs. Charles E. Cowan, *Steams in the Desert: Volume II* (United States: Cowan Publishing Company, Inc., 1966), September 22nd.
10. Dr. James Dobson, *Solid Answers* (Wheaton, Illinois: Tyndale House Publishers Inc., 1997), page 142-146.
11. Dr. James Dobson, *Dr. James answers Your Questions* (Wheaton, Illinois: Tyndale House Publishers, Inc., 1982), page 161.

Chapter 10

1. Fred H. Wight, *Manners and Customs of Bible Lands* (Chicago: Moody Press, 1953), pages 149-150.
2. Robert Gamble, *Shepherd My Sheep* (Belfast Northern Ireland/Greenville South Carolina: Ambassador publications, 1997), pages 76-81.
3. Phillip Keller, *A Shepherd looks at Psalm 23 {Large Print}* (Grand Rapids, Michigan: Zondervan Publishing House, 1970), pages 60, 99-103.
4. Phillip Keller, *A Shepherd looks at Psalm 23 {Large Print}* (Grand Rapids, Michigan: Zondervan Publishing House, 1970), pages 35-48, 114-126.
5. David Roper, *The Son of a Passionate Heart 23rd Psalm* (Grand Rapids, Michigan: Discovery Publishing House, 1994), pages 37-38.
6. Illumina Gold Incorporation/Visual Book Productions, *Thomas the Apostle* (Carol Stream, Illinois: Tyndale House Publications, 2003).

Chapter 14

1. Hartford Institute for Religion Research, *Fast Facts about American Religion/ What's the size of U.S. Churches* (Hartford, Connecticut, 2000-2006), Internet:hartsem.edu/ research/fast_facts.

Chapter 16

1. American College Dictionary, Edited by Barnhart, *Green-housing* (New York, Random House, 1963), page 530.
2. David Barton, *Education and the founding Fathers* (Aledo, Texas, Wall Builders Press, 1993), page 6.

Destinée Media

Destinée Media publishes both fiction and nonfiction and aims to bring a fresh perspective to spirituality and culture.

At Destinée Media we seek to operate by faith in God within a Biblical/Christian worldview. We hope to inspire 'culture-making' by promoting ideas that will contribute to Christ being understood as Lord of the whole of life, which is to be marked by redemption and renewal. We are committed to reflecting carefully on vital matters for the church, academy and society, while aiming to keep a personal and intimate dimension of the Christian life in view.

We thank you for your interest in our materials and hope that you find them both relevant and challenging. Please share your thoughts with us:

www.destineemedia.com

destinēe

CPSIA information can be obtained at www.ICGtesting.com
Printed in the USA
BVOW020153211112

306082BV00002B/2/P